I0454963

United States Government Accountability Office

GAO

Report to the Chairman, Select Committee on Energy Independence and Global Warming, House of Representatives

October 2009

CLIMATE CHANGE ADAPTATION

Strategic Federal Planning Could Help Government Officials Make More Informed Decisions

GAO-10-113

GAO
Accountability · Integrity · Reliability

Highlights

Highlights of GAO-10-113, a report to the Chairman, Select Committee on Energy Independence and Global Warming, House of Representatives

CLIMATE CHANGE ADAPTATION

Strategic Federal Planning Could Help Government Officials Make More Informed Decisions

Why GAO Did This Study

Changes in the climate attributable to increased concentrations of greenhouse gases may have significant impacts in the United States and the world. For example, climate change could threaten coastal areas with rising sea levels. Greenhouse gases already in the atmosphere will continue altering the climate system into the future, regardless of emissions control efforts. Therefore, adaptation—defined as adjustments to natural or human systems in response to actual or expected climate change—is an important part of the response to climate change.

GAO was asked to examine (1) what actions federal, state, local, and international authorities are taking to adapt to a changing climate; (2) the challenges that federal, state, and local officials face in their efforts to adapt; and (3) actions that Congress and federal agencies could take to help address these challenges. We also discuss our prior work on similarly complex, interdisciplinary issues. This report is based on analysis of studies, site visits to areas pursuing adaptation efforts, and responses to a Web-based questionnaire sent to federal, state, and local officials.

What GAO Recommends

GAO recommends that within the Executive Office of the President the appropriate entities, such as the Council on Environmental Quality (CEQ), develop a national adaptation plan that includes setting priorities for federal, state, and local agencies. CEQ generally agreed with our recommendations.

View GAO-10-113 or key components. To view the e-supplement online, click on GAO-10-114SP. For more information, contact John B. Stephenson at (202) 512-3841 or stephensonj@gao.gov.

What GAO Found

While available information indicates that many governments have not yet begun to adapt to climate change, some federal, state, local, and international authorities have started to act. For example, the U.S. National Oceanic and Atmospheric Administration's Regional Integrated Sciences and Assessments program supports research to meet the adaptation-related information needs of local decision makers. In another example, the state of Maryland's strategy for reducing vulnerability to climate change focuses on protecting habitat and infrastructure from future risks associated with sea level rise and coastal storms. Other GAO discussions with officials from New York City; King County, Washington; and the United Kingdom show how some governments have started to adapt to current and projected impacts in their jurisdictions.

The challenges faced by federal, state, and local officials in their efforts to adapt fell into three categories, based on GAO's analysis of questionnaire results, site visits, and available studies. First, competing priorities make it difficult to pursue adaptation efforts when there may be more immediate needs for attention and resources. For example, about 71 percent (128 of 180) of the officials who responded to our questionnaire rated "non-adaptation activities are higher priorities" as very or extremely challenging. Second, a lack of site-specific data, such as local projections of expected changes, can reduce the ability of officials to manage the effects of climate change. For example, King County officials noted that they are not sure how to translate climate data into effects on salmon recovery. Third, adaptation efforts are constrained by a lack of clear roles and responsibilities among federal, state, and local agencies. Of particular note, about 70 percent (124 of 178) of the respondents rated the "lack of clear roles and responsibilities for addressing adaptation across all levels of government" as very or extremely challenging.

GAO's analysis also found that potential federal actions for addressing challenges to adaptation efforts fell into three areas. First, training and education efforts could increase awareness among government officials and the public about the impacts of climate change and available adaptation strategies. Second, actions to provide and interpret site-specific information would help officials understand the impacts of climate change at a scale that would enable them to respond. For instance, about 80 percent (147 of 183) of the respondents rated the "development of state and local climate change impact and vulnerability assessments" as very or extremely useful. Third, Congress and federal agencies could encourage adaptation by clarifying roles and responsibilities. About 71 percent (129 of 181) of the respondents rated the development of a national adaptation strategy as very or extremely useful.

Climate change is a complex, interdisciplinary issue with the potential to affect every sector and level of government operations. Our past work on crosscutting issues suggests that governmentwide strategic planning—with the commitment of top leaders—can integrate activities that span a wide array of federal, state, and local entities.

_____ United States Government Accountability Office

Contents

Figures

Abbreviations

CDC	Centers for Disease Control and Prevention
CEQ	Council on Environmental Quality
CIG	Climate Impacts Group
DEFRA	Department for Environment, Food and Rural Affairs
DEP	Department of Environmental Protection
DNR	Department of Natural Resources
DNRP	Department of Natural Resources and Parks
DOT	U.S. Department of Transportation
EPA	U.S. Environmental Protection Agency
FEMA	Federal Emergency Management Agency
FWS	U.S. Fish and Wildlife Service
GCM	General Circulation Model
Interior	U.S. Department of the Interior
NAPA	National Adaptation Programme of Action
NASA	National Aeronautics and Space Administration
NIH	National Institutes of Health
NOAA	National Oceanic and Atmospheric Administration
NPCC	New York City Panel on Climate Change
NRC	National Research Council
RISA	Regional Integrated Sciences and Assessments
UKCIP	United Kingdom Climate Impacts Programme
USAID	U.S. Agency for International Development
USDA	U.S. Department of Agriculture
USGCRP	U.S. Global Change Research Program
USGS	U.S. Geological Survey

United States Government Accountability Office
Washington, DC 20548

October 7, 2009

The Honorable Edward Markey
Chairman
Select Committee on Energy Independence
    and Global Warming
House of Representatives

Dear Mr. Chairman:

Changes in the earth's climate attributable to increased concentrations of greenhouse gases may have significant environmental and economic impacts in the United States and internationally.[1] Among other potential impacts, climate change could threaten coastal areas with rising sea levels, alter agricultural productivity, and increase the intensity and frequency of floods and tropical storms. Federal, state, and local agencies are tasked with a wide array of responsibilities, such as managing natural resources, that will be affected by a changing climate. Furthermore, climate change has implications for the fiscal health of the federal government, affecting federal crop and flood insurance programs, and placing new stresses on infrastructure. The effects of increases in atmospheric concentrations of greenhouse gases and temperature on ecosystems are expected to vary across regions (see table 1).

---

[1]Major greenhouse gases include carbon dioxide (CO_2); methane (CH_4); nitrous oxide (N_2O); and synthetic gases such as hydrofluorocarbons (HFC), perfluorocarbons (PFC), and sulfur hexafluoride (SF_6).

Table 1: Current and Projected Impacts of Climate Change in the United States

Category	Current and projected impacts
Temperature	• U.S. average temperature has risen more than 2 degrees Fahrenheit over the past 50 years and is projected to rise more in the future—how much more depends primarily on the amount of heat-trapping gases emitted globally and how sensitive the climate is to those emissions.
Precipitation	• Precipitation has increased an average of about 5 percent over the past 50 years. Projections of future precipitation generally indicate that northern areas will become wetter and southern areas, particularly in the West, will become drier.
	• The amount of rain falling in the heaviest downpours has increased approximately 20 percent on average in the past century, and this trend is very likely to continue, with the largest increases in the wettest places.
Extreme weather events	• Many types of extreme weather events, such as heat waves and regional droughts, have become more frequent and intense during the past 40 to 50 years.
Storms	• The destructive energy of Atlantic hurricanes has increased in recent decades. The intensity of these storms is likely to increase in this century.
	• In the eastern Pacific, the strongest hurricanes have become stronger since the 1980s, even while the total number of storms has decreased.
	• Cold season storm tracks are shifting northward, and the strongest storms are likely to become stronger and more frequent.
Sea levels	• Sea level has risen along most of the U.S. coast over the last 50 years and will likely rise more in the future.
	• Arctic sea ice is declining rapidly and this decline is very likely to continue.

Source: Adapted from the U.S. Global Change Research Program, Global Climate Change Impacts in the United States, 2009.

Proposed responses to climate change include reducing greenhouse gas emissions through regulation, promoting low-emissions technologies, and adapting to the possible impacts by planning and improving protective infrastructure. Thus far, federal government attention and resources have been focused on emissions reduction options, climate science research, and technology investment. In recent years, however, climate change adaptation—adjustments to natural or human systems in response to actual or expected climate change—has begun to receive more attention because the greenhouse gases already in the atmosphere are expected to continue altering the climate system into the future, regardless of efforts to control emissions.

Policymakers are increasingly viewing adaptation as a risk-management strategy to protect vulnerable sectors and communities that might be affected by changes in the climate. As the Director of the Office of Science and Technology Policy in the Executive Office of the President stated in a 2009 testimony, we can invest in countless ways to reduce our vulnerability to the changes in climate that we do not succeed in avoiding, for example by breeding heat- and drought-resistant crop strains, bolstering our defenses against tropical diseases, improving the efficiency of our water use, and starting to manage our coastal zones with sea level rise in mind.[2] Furthermore, certain natural resource adaptation activities—such as efforts to build large, connected landscapes—will become more important as native species attempt to migrate or otherwise adapt to climate change. While it may be costly to raise river or coastal dikes to protect communities and resources from sea level rise, build higher bridges, or improve storm water systems, there is a growing recognition, in the United States and elsewhere, that the cost of inaction could be greater.

According to a recent report by the National Research Council (NRC), however, individuals and institutions whose futures will be affected by climate change are unprepared both conceptually and practically for meeting the challenges and opportunities it presents. Many usual practices and decision rules (for building bridges, implementing zoning rules, using private motor vehicles, and so on) assume a stationary climate—a continuation of past climate conditions, including similar patterns of variation and the same probabilities of extreme events. According to NRC, that assumption, fundamental to the ways people and organizations make their choices, is no longer valid.

Adapting to climate change requires making policy and management decisions that cut across traditional economic sectors, agencies, jurisdictional boundaries, and levels of government. The authorities and expertise necessary to facilitate adaptation activities are spread among many agencies. Recent proposed legislation considers governmentwide adaptation strategies, including the development of a National Climate Service to inform the public through the sustained production and delivery of authoritative, timely, and useful information about the impacts of climate change on local, state, regional, tribal, national, and global scales.[3] For example, the American Clean Energy and Security Act of 2009, which passed the House of Representatives on June 26, 2009, contains provisions related to climate change adaptation, including the development of federal and state natural resource agency adaptation plans and the establishment of a natural resources climate change adaptation fund.

---

[2]Statement of Dr. John P. Holdren, Director, Office of Science and Technology, Executive Office of the President before the Committee on Agriculture, United States Senate (Washington, D.C., July 22, 2009).

[3]See, e.g., National Climate Service Act of 2009, H.R. 2306, 111th Congress (2009); American Clean Energy and Security Act of 2009, H.R. 2454, 111th Congress (2009); National Climate Service Act of 2009, H.R. 2407, 111th Congress (2009).

In this context, our review (1) determines what actions, if any, federal, state, local, and international authorities are taking to adapt to a changing climate; (2) identifies the challenges, if any, that federal, state, and local officials reported facing in their efforts to adapt; and (3) identifies actions that Congress and federal agencies could take to help address these challenges. We also provide information about our prior work on similarly complex, interdisciplinary issues.

To determine the actions federal, state, local, and international authorities are taking to adapt to a changing climate, we obtained summaries of adaptation-related efforts from a broad range of federal agencies and visited four sites where government officials are taking actions to adapt.[4] We chose these sites because they were frequently mentioned in the background literature and scoping interviews as examples of locations that are implementing climate change adaptation and which may offer particularly useful insights into the types of actions governments can take to plan for climate change impacts. The four sites were New York City; King County, Washington; the state of Maryland; and the United Kingdom. Our selected sites are not representative of all adaptation efforts taking place; however, they include a variety of responses to climate change effects across different levels of government. We included an international site visit to examine how other countries are also starting to adapt. We gathered information during and after site visits through observation of adaptation efforts, interviews with officials and stakeholders, and a review of documents provided by these officials.

To describe challenges that federal, state, and local officials face in their efforts to adapt and the actions that Congress and federal agencies could take to help address these challenges, we reviewed available studies and asked knowledgeable stakeholders about challenges that federal, state, and local officials may face in adaptation efforts. Using this information, we compiled lists of potential challenges and potential actions the federal government could take to address them and developed a Web-based questionnaire to gather officials' views on these challenges and actions. We designed the questionnaire to collect aggregate information through a range of closed-ended questions, as well as illustrative examples through open-ended responses. Within the questionnaire, we organized questions about challenges and actions into groups related to the following: (1)

---

[4]Information on selected federal efforts to adapt to climate change is provided in a supplement to this report (see GAO-10-114SP).

awareness and priorities, (2) information, and (3) the structure and operation of the federal government. We worked with organizations that represent federal, state, and local officials to select a nonprobability sample of 274 officials knowledgeable about adaptation, of which 187 completed the questionnaire, for a response rate of approximately 68 percent.[5] The federal, state, and local officials who responded represent a diverse array of disciplines, including planners, scientists, and public health professionals. A more detailed description of our scope and methodology is available in appendix I.

We conducted this performance audit from September 2008 to October 2009 in accordance with generally accepted government auditing standards. Those standards require that we plan and perform the audit to obtain sufficient, appropriate evidence to provide a reasonable basis for our findings and conclusions based on our audit objectives. We believe that the evidence obtained provides a reasonable basis for our findings and conclusions based on our audit objectives.

Federal, State, Local, and International Efforts to Adapt to Climate Change

While federal agencies are beginning to recognize the need to adapt to climate change, there is a general lack of strategic coordination across agencies, and most efforts to adapt to potential climate change impacts are preliminary. However, some states and localities have begun to make progress on adaptation independently and through partnerships with other entities, such as academic institutions. The subjects of our site visits in the United States—New York City; King County, Washington; and Maryland—have all taken steps to plan for climate change and have begun to implement adaptive measures in sectors such as natural resource management and infrastructure. Their on-the-ground experiences can help inform the federal approach to adaptation, which is now primarily focused on assessing projected climate impacts and exploring adaptation options. In addition, certain nations have taken action to adapt to climate change. Our detailed examination of the United Kingdom provides an example of a country where central and local government entities are working together to address climate change impacts.

---

[5]Not all officials responded to every question.

Many Federal Agencies Are Beginning to Take Steps to Adapt to Climate Change

Although there is no coordinated national approach to adaptation, several federal agencies report that they have begun to take action with current and planned adaptation activities. These activities are largely ad hoc and fall into several categories, including (1) information for decision making, (2) federal land and natural resource management, (3) infrastructure design and operation, (4) public health research, (5) national security preparation, (6) international assistance to developing countries, and (7) governmentwide adaptation strategies. We provide information on selected federal efforts to adapt to climate change, submitted to us by federal agencies, in a supplement to this report (see GAO-10-114SP).

Information for decision making: A range of preliminary adaptation-related activities are reported to be under way at different agencies, including efforts to provide relevant climate information to help decision makers plan for future climate impacts. For example, two programs managed by the National Oceanic and Atmospheric Administration (NOAA) help policymakers and managers obtain the information they need to adapt to a changing climate. NOAA's Regional Integrated Sciences and Assessments (RISA) program supports climate change research to meet the needs of decision makers and policy planners at the national, regional, and local levels. Similarly, NOAA's Sectoral Applications Research Program is designed to help decision makers in different sectors, such as coastal resource managers, use climate information to respond to and plan for climate variability and change, among other goals.

Other agencies—including the National Science Foundation, the Department of the Interior (Interior), the Environmental Protection Agency (EPA), the National Aeronautics and Space Administration (NASA), and the Department of Energy—also manage programs to provide climate information to decision makers. For example, the National Science Foundation supports the scientific research needed to help authorities and the public plan adaptation activities and address any challenges that arise. Similarly, Interior's newly formed Energy and Climate Change Task Force is working to ensure that climate change impact data collection and analysis are better integrated and disseminated, that data gaps are identified and filled, and that the translation of science into adaptive management techniques is geared to the needs of land, water, and wildlife managers as they develop adaptation strategies in response to climate change-induced impacts on landscapes. Another example of information sharing is EPA's Climate Ready Estuaries program, which provides a toolkit to coastal communities and participants in its National Estuary Program on how to monitor climate change and where to find data. In addition, NASA's Applied Sciences Program is working in 31 states and with a number of federal agencies to help officials use NASA's climate data to make adaptation decisions. For example, NASA forecasts stream temperatures for NOAA managers responsible for managing chinook salmon populations in the Sacramento River and predicts water flow regimes and subsequent fire risk in Yosemite National Park. DOE's Integrated Assessment Research Program supports research on models and tools for integrated analysis of both the drivers and consequences of climate change. DOE's supercomputing resources provide the capability to assess impacts and vulnerabilities to temperature change, anticipate extreme events, and predict risk from climate change effects (e.g., water availability) on a regional and local basis to better inform decision makers.

Federal land and natural resource management: Several federal agencies have reported beginning to consider measures that would strengthen the resilience of natural resources in the face of climate change. For example, on September 14, 2009, Interior issued an order designed to address the impacts of climate change on the nation's water, land, and other natural and cultural resources.[6] The Interior order, among other things, designated eight regional Climate Change Response Centers. According to Interior, these centers will synthesize existing climate change impact data and management strategies, help resource managers put them into action on the ground, and engage the public through education initiatives. Similarly, several federal agencies recently released draft reports required by Presidential Executive Order that describe strategies for protecting and restoring the Chesapeake Bay, including addressing the impacts of climate change on the bay.[7] In addition, the U.S. Forest Service reported that it devotes about $9 million to adaptation research and has developed a strategic framework that recognizes the need to enhance the capacity of forests and grasslands to adapt. The Chief of the Forest Service recently testified that dealing with climate change risks and uncertainties will need

---

[6]Secretarial Order No. 3289 (Sep. 14, 2009).

[7]The Executive Order required the U.S. Department of Agriculture, U.S. Department of Defense, EPA, Interior, and the U.S. Department of Commerce to submit draft reports. Draft reports are available at http://executiveorder.chesapeakebay.net/.

to be a more prominent part of the Forest Service's management decision processes.[8]

Certain agencies have also identified specific adaptation strategies and tools for natural resource managers. For example, Interior provided a number of adaptation-related policy options for land managers in reports produced for its Climate Change Task Force, a past effort that has since been expanded upon to reflect new priorities.[9] Similarly, a recent U.S. Climate Change Science Program report provided a preliminary review of adaptation options for climate-sensitive ecosystems and resources on federally owned and managed lands.[10] In addition, the Department of Defense's Legacy Resource Management Program is working with other agencies to develop a guidance manual that will summarize available natural resource vulnerability assessment tools.

In some instances, federal agencies have begun to help implement adaptation actions. A recent Congressional Research Service presentation highlighted two case studies on federal lands in which federal agencies assisted with adaptation efforts. The first is a habitat restoration project supported by the U.S. Fish and Wildlife Service (FWS) to adapt to sea level rise in the Albemarle Peninsula, North Carolina. The second focuses on increasing landscape diversity and managing biodiversity in Washington's Olympic National Forest, the site of a Forest Service Pacific Northwest Research Station. The project involved work with the Federal Highway Administration to protect watersheds and roads.[11] In addition, the

---

[8]*The Role of Federal Lands in Combating Climate Change: Hearing Before the Subcommittee on National Parks, Forests, and Public Lands of the House Committee on Natural Resources*, 111th Cong. 7-12 (2009) (written statement of Abigail Kimbell, Chief, U.S. Forest Service). Also, on January 16, 2009, the Forest Service issued guidance for addressing climate change considerations in land management planning and project implementation.

[9]For more information about Interior's Climate Change Task Force, see http://www.usgs.gov/global_change/doi_taskforce.asp.

[10]The Climate Change Science Program is now referred to as the United States Global Change Research Program. For report citation, see S.H. Julius, J.M. West (eds.), J.S. Baron, B. Griffith, L.A. Joyce, P. Kareiva, B.D. Keller, M.A. Palmer, C.H. Peterson, and J.M. Scott, *Preliminary Review of Adaptation Options for Climate-Sensitive Ecosystems and Resources*, Final Report, Synthesis and Assessment Product 4.4 (SAP 4.4), a report for the U.S. Climate Change Science Program and the Subcommittee on Global Change Research, U.S. Environmental Protection Agency, Washington, D.C., 2008.

[11]M.L. Corn, R.W. Gorte, G. Siekaniec, M. Bryan, D. Cleaves, K. O'Halloran, *Global Climate Change and Federal Lands: Two Cases*, a presentation hosted by the Congressional Research Service, 2009.

Department of Energy reported that it has assessed major water availability issues related to energy production and use, such as electrical generation and fuels production, and identified approaches that could reduce freshwater use in the energy sector, and opportunities for further research and development to address questions that decision makers will need to resolve to effectively manage the energy and water availability issues.

Infrastructure design and operation: A number of federal agencies are beginning to recognize that they must account for climate change impacts when building and repairing man-made infrastructure, since such impacts have implications beyond the natural environment.[12] Many adaptation efforts related to infrastructure are at the planning stages to date. For example, the U.S. Army Corps of Engineers' adaptation initiatives include leading a team of water managers to evaluate how climate change considerations can be incorporated into activities related to water resources. These managers are also participating in an interagency group (Climate Change and Water Working Group) which held workshops in California in spring 2007. At these workshops, water managers from federal (U.S. Geological Survey (USGS), Bureau of Reclamation, NOAA), state, local, and private agencies and organizations recommended more flexible reservoir operations, better use of forecasts, and more monitoring of real-time conditions in the watersheds. A draft report of long-term needs identified by the team was undergoing agency review in August and September 2009. In addition, EPA recently issued a guide entitled *Smart Growth for Coastal and Waterfront Communities* to help communities address challenges such as potential sea level rise and other climate-related hazards.[13]

Within the U.S. Department of Transportation (DOT), the Federal Highway Administration also formed a multidisciplinary internal working group to coordinate infrastructure policy and program activities, specifically to

---

[12]In technical comments to this report, Interior pointed out that there are significant links between federal land and natural resource management and infrastructure design and operation. According to Interior, proper management of lands and natural resources can help protect human infrastructure and can be an adaptation strategy for human infrastructure in and of itself. For example, restoring coastal wetlands can help protect human infrastructure against storm surges, rising sea level, and erosion.

[13]EPA developed this guide in conjunction with NOAA, Rhode Island Sea Grant, and the International City/County Management Association. See http://coastalsmartgrowth.noaa.gov/.

address climate change effects on transportation. Both the U.S. Army Corps of Engineers and DOT are reviewing the impacts of sea level rise on infrastructure. DOT found that a 2-foot sea level rise would affect 64 percent of the Gulf Coast's port facilities, while a 4-foot rise would affect nearly three-quarters of port facilities.[14] In addition, the Federal Emergency Management Agency (FEMA), part of the U.S. Department of Homeland Security, is currently conducting a study on the impact of climate change on the National Flood Insurance Program, as we recommended in a 2007 GAO report.[15] The Department of Energy is also working to protect critical infrastructure—such as the national laboratories and the Strategic Petroleum Reserve—by using climate impact assessments and developing guidance for management decisions that account for climate change.

Public health research: Federal agencies responsible for public health matters are starting to support modeling and research efforts to assess climate change impacts on their programs and issue areas. Currently, the Centers for Disease Control and Prevention's (CDC) Climate Change program is engaged in a number of adaptation initiatives that address various populations' vulnerability to the adverse health effects of heat waves. For example, CDC helped develop a Web-based modeling tool to assist local and regional governments to prepare for heat waves and an extreme heat media toolkit for cities.

In addition, the National Institutes of Health (NIH) formed a working group on Climate Change and Health, which aims to identify research needs and priorities and involve the biomedical research community in discussions of the health effects of climate change. Recently, NIH developed an initiative called the NIH Challenge Grants in Health and Science Research, which supports research on predictive climate change models and facilitates public health planning. Of particular interest to NIH are studies that quantify the current impacts of climate on a variety of communicable or noncommunicable diseases or studies that project the impacts of different climate and socioeconomic scenarios on health.

---

[14]M. J. Savonis, V.R. Burkett, and J.R. Potter (eds.), *Impacts of Climate Change and Variability on Transportation Systems and Infrastructure: Gulf Coast Study, Phase I*, Synthesis and Assessment Product 4.7 (SAP 4.4), a report for the U.S. Climate Change Science Program and the Subcommittee on Global Change Research, U.S. Department of Transportation, Washington, D.C., 2008.

[15]GAO, *Climate Change: Financial Risks to Federal and Private Insurers in Coming Decades Are Potentially Significant*, GAO-07-285 (Washington, D.C.: Mar. 16, 2007).

EPA is also taking steps to ensure that public health needs are met in the context of climate change. For example, EPA helped produce an analysis that examined potential impacts of climate change on human society, opportunities for adaptation, and associated recommendations for addressing data gaps and research goals.[16] In addition, EPA is working with agencies such as CDC, NIH, and NOAA to support the public health communities' efforts to develop strategies for adapting to climate change.

National security preparation: Federal agencies are beginning to study the potential consequences of climate change on national security. For example, the Department of Defense's ongoing Quadrennial Defense Review is examining the capabilities of the armed forces to respond to the consequences of climate change—in particular, preparedness for natural disasters from extreme weather events, as is required by Section 951 of the National Defense Authorization Act for fiscal year 2008.[17] This act also requires the department to develop guidance for military planners to assess the risk of projected climate change, update defense plans based on these assessments, and develop the capabilities needed to reduce future impacts. In October 2008, the Air Force participated in a Colloquium on National Security Implications of Climate Change sponsored by the U.S. Joint Forces Command. In addition, the Navy recently sponsored a Naval Studies Board study on the National Security Implications of Climate Change on U.S. Naval forces (Navy, Marine Corps, and Coast Guard), to be completed in late 2010. This study is intended to help the Navy develop future robust climate change adaptation strategies.

International assistance to developing countries: Some federal agencies are supporting preliminary adaptation planning efforts internationally. For example, the U.S. Agency for International Development (USAID) funds climate change activities related to agriculture, water, forest, and coastal zone management in partner developing countries. To inform such activities, USAID produced two documents, an adaptation guidance manual and a coastal zone adaptation manual, which provide climate

---

[16]J.L. Gamble (ed.), K.L. Ebi, F.G. Sussman, T.J. Wilbanks, *Analyses of the Effects of Global Change on Human Health and Welfare and Human Systems*, Synthesis and Assessment Product 4.6 (SAP 4.6), a report for the U.S. Climate Change Science Program and the Subcommittee on Global Change Research, U.S. Environmental Protection Agency, Washington, D.C., 2008.

[17]National Defense Authorization Act for Fiscal Year 2008, Pub. L. No. 110-181, § 951, 122 Stat. 290 (2008).

change tools and other information to planners in the developing world.[18] In addition, USAID works with NASA to provide developing countries with climate change data to help support adaptation activities. For example, the two agencies use SERVIR, a high-tech regional satellite visualization and monitoring system for Central America, to provide a climate change scenario database, climate change maps indicating impacts on Central America's biodiversity, a fire and smoke mapping and warning system, red tide alerts, and weather alerts. The U.S. Department of State's and NOAA's climate efforts also sustain adaptation initiatives worldwide. NOAA is supporting USAID programs in Asia, Latin America, and Africa by using a science-based approach to enhance governments' abilities to understand, anticipate, and manage climate risk. In addition, Interior's International Technical Assistance Program, funded through interagency agreements with USAID and the U.S. Department of State, provides training and technical assistance to developing countries.[19]

Governmentwide adaptation strategies: Currently, no single entity is coordinating climate change adaptation efforts across the federal government and there is a general lack of strategic coordination. However, several federal entities are beginning to develop governmentwide strategies to adapt to climate change. For example, the President's Council on Environmental Quality (CEQ) is leading a new initiative to coordinate the federal response to climate change in conjunction with the Office of Science and Technology Policy, NOAA, and other agencies. Similarly, the U.S. Global Change Research Program (USGCRP), which coordinates and integrates federal research on climate change, has developed a series of "building blocks" that outline options for future climate change work,

---

[18]USAID, *Adapting to Climate Variability and Change: A Guidance Manual for Development Planning* (August 2007) and *Adapting to Coastal Climate Change: A Guidebook for Development Planners* (May 2009).

[19]In technical comments to this report, Interior also cited other programs that can assist in international adaptation, including (1) the Famine Early Warning System, which uses remote sensing to monitor floods and droughts in Africa, the Americas, and Afghanistan (USGS); (2) wildland fire cooperation with Mexico, Canada, Australia, and New Zealand (Bureau of Land Management, National Park Service, FWS, Bureau of Indian Affairs); (3) integrated water resource management, dam operations and safety, irrigation, flood control, water conservation in arid ecosystems, and hydrologic monitoring in Africa, Asia, and the Middle East (Bureau of Reclamation, USGS); (4) 30 sister park relationships with 20 countries that facilitate technical exchange and joint monitoring of protected ecosystems; (5) ecosystem monitoring, conservation of migratory and shared species with Mexico and Canada (FWS, National Park Service, Bureau of Land Management, USGS); and (6) conservation grants for elephants, rhinoceros, tigers, great apes, marine turtles, neotropical migratory birds, and waterfowl habitat (FWS).

including science to inform adaptation. The adaptation building block includes support and guidance for federal, regional, and local efforts to prepare for and respond to climate change, including characterizing the need for adaptation and developing, implementing, and evaluating adaptation approaches.

Certain State and Local Governments Are Developing and Implementing Climate Change Adaptation Measures

Many government authorities at the state and local levels have not yet begun to adapt to climate change. According to a recent NRC report, the response of governments at all levels, businesses and industries, and civil society is only starting, and much is still to be learned about the institutional, technological, and economic shifts that have begun.[20] Some states have not yet started to consider mitigation or adaptation; others have developed plans but have not yet begun to implement them. However, certain governments are beginning to plan for the effects of climate change and to implement climate change adaptation measures. For example, California recently issued a draft climate adaptation strategy, which directs the state government to prepare for rising sea levels, increased wildfires, and other expected changes.[21] A general review of state and local government adaptation planning efforts is available in two recent reports issued by nongovernment research groups.[22]

We visited three U.S. sites—New York City; King County, Washington; and the state of Maryland—where government officials have begun to plan for and respond to climate change impacts. The three locations are all addressing climate change adaptation to various extents. New York City is in the planning phases for its citywide efforts, although individual

---

[20]National Research Council of the National Academies, Panel on Strategies and Methods for Climate-Related Decision Support, Committee on the Human Dimensions of Global Change, *Informing Decisions in a Changing Climate* (Washington, D.C., 2009).

[21]California Natural Resources Agency, *2009 California Climate Adaptation Strategy, Discussion Draft*.

[22]See Terri L. Cruce, *Adaptation Planning: What U.S. States and Localities are Doing*, a special report prepared for the Pew Center on Global Climate Change, November 2007 (updated August 2009), available at http://www.pewclimate.org/working-papers/adaptation and The H. John Heinz III Center for Science, Economics, and the Environment, *A Survey of Climate Change Adaptation Planning* (Washington, D.C., 2007), available at http://www.heinzctr.org/publications/meeting_reports.shtml. In addition, see Susanne C. Moser, *Good Morning, America! The Explosive U.S. Awakening to the Need for Adaptation*, a special report prepared at the request of the NOAA Coastal Services Center and the California Energy Commission, May 2009, available at http://www.csc.noaa.gov/publications/need-for-adaptation.pdf.

departments have begun to implement specific actions, such as purchasing land in New York City's watershed to improve the quality of its water supply. King County, Washington has, among other things, completed and begun to implement a comprehensive climate change plan, which includes an adaptation component. Maryland has released the first phase of its adaptation strategy, which is focused on sea level rise and coastal storms, reflecting sectors of immediate concern.

Our analysis of these sites suggests three major factors have led these governments to act. First, natural disasters such as floods, heat waves, droughts, or hurricanes raised public awareness of the costs of potential climate change impacts. Second, leaders in all three sites used legislation, executive orders, local ordinances, or action plans to focus attention and resources on climate change adaptation. Finally, each of the governments had access to relevant site-specific information to provide a basis for planning and management efforts. This site-specific information arose from partnerships that decision makers at all three sites formed with local universities and other government and nongovernment entities.

The following summaries describe the key factors that motivated these governments to act, the policies and laws that guide adaptation activities at each location, the programs and initiatives that are in place to address climate effects, the sources of site-specific information, and any partnerships that have assisted with adaptation activities.

New York City, New York

New York City's adaptation efforts stemmed from a growing recognition of the vulnerability of the city's infrastructure to natural disasters, such as the severe flooding in 2007 that led to widespread subway closures. The development of PlaNYC—a plan to accommodate a projected population growth of 1 million people, reduce citywide carbon emissions by 30 percent, and make New York City a greener, more sustainable city by 2030—also pushed city officials to think about the future, including the need for climate change adaptation. New York City's extensive coastline and dense urban infrastructure makes it vulnerable to sea level rise; flooding; and other extreme weather, including heatwaves, which could become more common as a result of climate change.

City officials took several steps to formalize a response to climate change. In 2008, the Mayor convened the New York City Panel on Climate Change (NPCC) to provide localized climate change projections and decision tools. The Mayor also invited public agencies and private companies to be part of the New York City Climate Change Adaptation Task Force, a public-private group charged with assessing climate effects on critical infrastructure and developing adaptation strategies to reduce these risks. The Office of Long-Term Planning and Sustainability, established by a local law in 2008, provides oversight of the city's adaptation efforts, which are part of PlaNYC.[23] In addition to citywide efforts, a number of municipal and regional agencies have begun to address climate change adaptation in their operations.

To date, New York City's adaptation efforts typically have been implemented as facilities are upgraded or as funding becomes available. For example, the city's Department of Environmental Protection (DEP), which manages water and wastewater infrastructure, has begun to address flood risks to its wastewater treatment facilities. These and other efforts are described in DEP's *2008 Climate Change Program Assessment and Action Plan.*[24] Many of New York City's wastewater treatment plants, such as Tallman Island (see fig. 1) are vulnerable to sea level rise and flooding from storm surges because they are located in the floodplain next to the waterbodies into which they discharge. In response to this threat, DEP is, in the course of scheduled renovations, raising sensitive electrical equipment, such as pumps and motors, to higher levels to protect them from flood damage.

---

[23]Local Law No. 17 (2008) of City of New York, § 2.

[24]New York City Department of Environmental Protection Climate Change Program, with contributions by Columbia University's Center for Climate Systems Research and HydroQual Environmental Engineers & Scientists, P.C., *Report 1: Assessment and Action Plan—A Report Based on the Ongoing Work of the DEP Climate Change Task Force* (New York City, N.Y., 2008).

Figure 1: Tallman Island Water Pollution Control Plant, Queens, New York City

Source: GAO.

The Tallman Island Water Pollution Control Plant, located on the bank of the East River, is vulnerable to flooding due to storm surges and sea level rise.

Other municipal departments are implementing climate change adaptation measures as well. For example, the Department of Parks and Recreation launched a pilot project in its Five Borough Technical Services Facility to experiment with different types of green roofs—vegetated plots on rooftops that absorb rainwater and moderate the effects of heatwaves (see fig. 2). According to an official at the Department of Parks and Recreation, the department plans to install green roofs in some of its recreation facilities in the next few years, since these facilities will be replacing their roofs. Green roofs are part of a suite of measures the city is exploring to control stormwater at the source (the location where the rain falls), rather than pipe it elsewhere. This can help reduce the need for more infrastructure investments in preparation for more intense rainstorms—investments that can be very costly and that are not always feasible in the space available under the city streets.

Source: GAO.

Sedum (left) and native plants (right) are used in the green roof at the Five Borough Technical Services Facility.

New York City's adaptation efforts have benefited from officials' access to site-specific information, starting with the publication of a 2001 report for USGCRP, which provided a scientific assessment of climate change effects in the New York City metropolitan region.[25] More recently, the city, through the financial support of the Rockefeller Foundation, created NPCC. According to its co-chairs, NPCC is charged with completing several decision-support documents, which will provide decision makers with information about local climate effects.[26] In addition, the Mayor convened the New York City Climate Change Adaptation Task Force to prepare a risk-based assessment of how climate change would affect the communication, energy, water and waste, transportation, and policy sectors, as well as the urban ecosystem and parks, and prioritize potential response strategies. Members of the task force, several of whom represent private industries, explained that they agreed to participate in the task

[25]Columbia Earth Institute, *Climate Change and a Global City: the Potential Consequences of Climate Variability and Change Metro East Coast*, a special report prepared at the request of the U.S. Global Change Research Program, July 2001.

[26]The first of these documents has been released. See NPCC, *Climate Risk Information* (New York City, N.Y., 2009).

force because the Mayor made this issue a priority. They noted that events such as Hurricane Katrina in 2005; the power outage in August 2003, which affected New York City as well as other locations in the United States and Canada; and the 2007 subway flooding raised their awareness about the effects of climate change on their operations.

New York City partners with other state and local governments to share knowledge and implement climate change adaptation efforts. It is a charter member of the C40, a coalition of large cities around the world committed to addressing climate change. City agencies also share information with counterparts in other locations about specific concerns. For example, DEP shares information about addressing water-related climate change effects with the state of California and the Water Utility Climate Alliance, a national coalition of water and wastewater utilities. DEP coordinates with other state and local governments to address climate change effects on its watershed, which is located outside of city limits. Similarly, transportation agencies that serve New York City, such as the Metropolitan Transit Authority and New Jersey Transit, cross local and state boundaries and require coordination on a regional scale, which New York City addresses through its multijurisdictional task force. City officials and members of NPCC stated that a coherent federal response would further facilitate the development of common objectives across local and state jurisdictions.

King County, Washington

According to officials from the King County Department of Natural Resources and Parks (DNRP), the county took steps to adapt to climate change because its leadership was highly aware of climate impacts on the county and championed the need to take action. The county commissioned an internal study in 2005 that included each department's projection of its operations in 2050, which focused attention on the need to prepare for future climate changes. The county also sponsored a conference in 2005 that brought together scientists, local and state officials, the private sector, and the public to discuss the impacts of climate change.[27] This conference served to educate the public and officials and spur action.

---

[27]Lia Ossiander and Kevin Rennert, "Impacts of Climate Change on Washington State: Summary of Plenary Sessions" (prepared for *The Future Ain't What it Used to Be: Planning for Climate Disruption* conference in 2005, sponsored by King County, Seattle, Wash., October 2005).

GAO-10-113 Climate Change Adaptation

Officials from DNRP noted that recent weather events increased the urgency of certain adaptive actions. For example, in November 2006, the county experienced severe winter storms that caused a series of levees to crack. The levees had long needed repair, but the storm damage helped increase support for the establishment of a countywide flood control zone district, funded by a dedicated property tax.[28] The flood control zone district will use the funds, in part, to upgrade flood protection facilities, which will increase the county's resilience to future flooding. In addition to more severe winter storms, the county expects that climate change will lead to sea level rise; reduced snowpack; and summertime extreme weather such as heat waves and drought, which can lead to power shortages because hydropower is an important source of power in the region.

The county's first formal step toward adaptation was a climate change plan developed in 2007.[29] The county executive also issued several executive orders that call for, among other things, the evaluation of climate impacts in the State Environmental Policy Act reviews conducted by county departments and the consideration of global warming adaptation in county operations, such as transportation, waste and wastewater infrastructure, and land use planning.[30] For example, King County officials told us that during the construction of the Brightwater wastewater treatment plant, DNRP's Wastewater Treatment Division added a pipeline that could convey approximately 7 million gallons per day of reclaimed water to industrial and agricultural users upon completion in 2011. They also said that additional reclaimed water could be made available in the future as the need arises. The division is also addressing the effects of sea level rise by, for example, increasing the elevation of vulnerable facilities during design and installing flaps to prevent backflow into its pipelines. Additionally, in 2008, the county incorporated

[28]King County Ordinance 15728 (Apr. 25, 2007). The district is funded by a countywide ad valorem property tax levy of 10 cents per $1,000 assessed value.

[29]King County, *2007 Climate Plan* (Seattle, Wash., 2007).

[30]*See* King County Exec. Order No. PUT 7-8 (Mar. 22, 2006) (Executive Order on Land Use Strategies for Global Warming Preparedness); King County Exec. Order No. PUT 7-7 (Mar. 22, 2006) (Executive Order on Environmental Management Strategies for Global Warming Preparedness); King County Exec. Order No. PUT 7-10-1 (Aug. 31, 2007) (Evaluation of Climate Change Impacts through the State Environmental Policy Act).

GAO-10-113 Climate Change Adaptation

consideration of climate change into the revision of its Comprehensive Plan, which guides land use decisions throughout the county.[31]

King County officials told us that each county department convened internal teams that identify climate change initiatives and report to the King County Executive Action Group on Climate Change on their progress. For example, the county's Department of Transportation Road Services Division started a Climate Change Team in 2008, which identified several initiatives in response to projections for more intense storms, including investigating new approaches to stormwater treatment. Specifically, the Road Services Division is piloting a roadside rain garden, which captures and filters rainwater using vegetation and certain types of soil, to determine whether more of such installations could improve the onsite management of stormwater runoff, as compared to a traditional engineering approach, which would pipe the water to a pond or holding vault and then discharge it to an offsite waterbody (see fig. 3). Alongside the rain garden, a permeable concrete sidewalk will absorb additional rain that would normally flow off a traditional impervious sidewalk into adjacent property. The rain garden and permeable sidewalk are considered examples of "low-impact development," which are expected to help the county adapt to increased rainfall by reducing peak surface water flows from road surfaces by about 33 percent. The Road Services Division is also implementing other measures that could improve its response to storms, such as installing larger culverts, improving its ability to detect hazardous road conditions (for example, due to flooding), and communicating those conditions to maintenance staff and the general public.

[31]King County, *King County Comprehensive Plan 2008* (October 2008).

Figure 3: Rain Garden in King County, Washington

Source: King County Department of Transportation Road Services Division.

This rain garden, which is under construction, treats roadway runoff using natural vegetation and certain types of soil.

County officials receive information on climate change effects from a number of sources. The University of Washington Climate Impacts Group (CIG), funded by NOAA's RISA program, has had a long-standing relationship with county officials and works closely with them to provide regionally specific climate change data and modeling, such as a 2009 assessment of climate impacts in Washington, as well as decision-making tools.[32] For example, the CIG Web site provides a Climate Change Streamflow Scenario Tool, which allows water planners in the Columbia River basin to compare historical records with climate change scenarios. Similarly, according to its faculty, the Washington State University

---

[32]University of Washington Climate Impacts Group, *The Washington Climate Change Impacts Assessment: Evaluating Washington's Future in a Changing Climate* (Seattle, Wash., 2009).

Extension Office works with the county and CIG to provide climate change information to the agricultural and forestry sectors, both of which will be increasingly affected by insect infestation due to increases in temperatures. The university's Extension Office also provides direct technical assistance to landowners affected by these impacts. King County officials, according to the director of DNRP, also share information about climate change adaptation with other localities through several partnership efforts, including the Center for Clean Air Policy Urban Leaders Adaptation Initiative.

Maryland

The Secretary of the Maryland Department of Natural Resources (DNR) told us that Maryland began to work on climate change adaptation because of the state's vulnerability to coastal flooding due to sea level rise and severe storms. The Maryland coastline is particularly vulnerable due to a combination of global sea level rise and local land subsidence, or sinking, among other factors. It has already experienced a sea level rise of about 1 foot in the last 100 years, which led to the disappearance of 13 Chesapeake Bay islands. According to a recent state report, a 2- to 3-foot sea level rise could submerge thousands of acres of tidal wetlands; low-lying lands; and Smith Island in the Chesapeake Bay.[33] These ongoing concerns, along with widespread flooding caused by Hurricane Isabel in 2003, have increased awareness of climate change effects in the state.

Maryland officials have taken a number of steps to formalize their response to climate change effects. An executive order in 2007 established the Maryland Commission on Climate Change, which released the Maryland Climate Action Plan in 2008.[34] As part of this effort, DNR chaired an Adaptation and Response Working Group, which issued a report on sea level rise and coastal storms.[35] The 2008 Maryland Climate Action Plan calls for future adaptation strategy development to cover other sectors such as agriculture and human health.

---

[33]Maryland Commission on Climate Change Adaptation and Response Working Group, *Comprehensive Strategy for Reducing Maryland's Vulnerability to Climate Change Phase I: Sea Level Rise and Coastal Storms* (Annapolis, Md., 2008).

[34]Maryland Commission on Climate Change, *Climate Action Plan* (Annapolis, Md., 2008).

[35]Maryland Commission on Climate Change Adaptation and Response Working Group, *Comprehensive Strategy for Reducing Maryland's Vulnerability to Climate Change Phase I: Sea Level Rise and Coastal Storms.*

Maryland also enacted several legislative measures that address coastal concerns, including the Living Shoreline Protection Act of 2008, which generally requires the use of nonstructural shoreline stabilization measures instead of "hard" structures such as bulkheads and retaining walls (see fig. 4).[36] According to a Maryland official, as sea level rises there will be a greater need for shore protection. Living shorelines provide such protection, while also maintaining coastal processes and providing aquatic habitat. The Chesapeake and Atlantic Coastal Bays Critical Area Protection law was also amended to, among other things, require the state to update the maps used to determine the boundary of the critical areas at least once every 12 years.[37] Previously, the critical areas were based on a map drawn in 1972 that did not reflect changes caused by sea level rise or other coastal erosion processes.

---

[36]2008 Md. Laws 304, *codified at* Md. Envir. § 16-201.

[37]2008 Md. Laws 119, *codified at* Md. Nat. Res. § 8-1807. Critical areas are determined by local jurisdictions and approved by the Critical Area Commission for the Chesapeake and Atlantic Coastal Bays, but the initial planning area included all waters and lands under the Chesapeake Bay and Atlantic Coastal Bays and their tributaries and all land and water areas within 1,000 feet beyond the landward boundaries of state or private wetlands and heads of tides.

Figure 4: A Living Shoreline, Annapolis, Maryland

Source: GAO.

This living shoreline uses marsh plants and other natural features to protect the shore from erosion.

According to officials from DNR, the department is modifying several existing programs to ensure that the state is taking the effects of climate change into account. For example, an official from DNR told us that it is incorporating climate change into its ranking criteria for state land conservation. Specifically, this official said that DNR plans to prioritize coastal habitat for potential acquisition according to its suitability for marsh migration, among other factors. Additionally, Maryland is providing guidance to coastal counties to assist them with incorporating the effects of climate change into their planning documents. For example, DNR funded guidance documents to three coastal counties, Dorchester, Somerset, and Worcester Counties, on how to address sea level rise and other coastal hazards in their local ordinances and planning efforts.[38] Furthermore, in spring 2009, DNR officials participated in a public Somerset County sea level rise workshop designed to raise the awareness of county residents. Officials discussed what sea level rise projections could mean to the county, including the inundation of some of its coastal infrastructure and salt marsh habitat (see fig. 5), and described some of the state initiatives to address these effects. Finally, officials with the DNR Monitoring and Non-Tidal Assessment Division told us they are considering expanding their monitoring of sentinel sites—pristine streams where changing conditions can help detect localized impacts of climate change.

---

[38]Wanda Diane Cole, Maryland Eastern Shore Resource Conservation & Development Council, *Sea Level Rise: Technical Guidance for Dorchester County*, a special report prepared at the request of the Maryland Department of Natural Resources, March 2008; URS and RCQuinn Consulting, Inc., *Somerset County Maryland Rising Sea Level Guidance*, a special report prepared at the request of Somerset County, Maryland, Annapolis, Md., 2008; and CSA International Inc., *Sea Level Rise Response Strategy Worcester County, Maryland*, a special report prepared at the request of Worcester County, Maryland Department of Comprehensive Planning, September 2008.

Figure 5: Salt Marsh in Somerset County, Maryland

Source: GAO.

Salt marshes in Somerset County provide important habitat to migrating waterfowl and other species; they are at risk of inundation due to sea level rise.

Maryland draws on local universities, federal agencies, and others to access information relevant to climate change. For example, in 2008, scientists from the University of Maryland chaired and participated in the Scientific and Technical Working Group of the Maryland Commission on Climate Change. Faculty from the University of Maryland also provide technical information to the state government and legislature on an ongoing basis. Maryland receives grants and additional technical assistance from the federal government and collaborates with federal agencies and local universities to collect and disseminate data relevant to climate change adaptation. Specifically, Maryland used local, state, and federal resources to map its coastline using Light Detection and Ranging technology and has made this information, as well as a number of tools that can be used by the public and decision makers, readily available in the

Maryland Shorelines Online Web site.[39] For example, an interactive mapping application called Shoreline Changes Online allows users to access historic shoreline data to determine erosion trends.[40]

Some Countries Have Begun to Adapt to Climate Change

Limited adaptation efforts are also taking root in other countries around the world. In 2007, the Intergovernmental Panel on Climate Change's Fourth Assessment Report found that some adaptation measures are being implemented in both developing and developed countries, but that many of these measures are in the preliminary stages.[41] As in the case of the state and local efforts described earlier, some of these adaptation efforts have been triggered by the recognition that current weather extremes and seasonal changes will become more frequent in the future. For example, recognizing the hazards of rising temperatures, efforts are under way in Nepal to drain the expanding Tsho Rolpa glacial lake to reduce flood risk. Similarly, in response to reduced snow cover and glacial retreat, the winter tourism industry in the European Alpine region has implemented a number of measures, such as building reservoirs to support artificial snowmaking.

A number of countries have begun to assess their vulnerability to climate change impacts and formulate national responses. For example, Canada issued a report in 2008 that discusses the current and future risks and opportunities that climate change presents, primarily from a regional perspective.[42] Australia recently issued guidance to local governments about expected climate change projections, impacts, and potential responses.[43] In addition, under the United Nations Framework Convention on Climate Change, least-developed countries can receive funding to develop National Adaptation Programmes of Action (NAPA)—38 NAPAs

---

[39]See http://shorelines.dnr.state.md.us. *Maryland Shorelines Online* is a coastal hazards Web portal, centralizing information and data on shoreline and coastal hazards management in Maryland.

[40]See http://shorelines.dnr.state.md.us/sc_online.asp.

[41]Intergovernmental Panel on Climate Change, *Climate Change 2007: Impacts, Adaptation and Vulnerability, Contribution of Working Group II to the Fourth Assessment Report of the Intergovernmental Panel on Climate Change* (Cambridge, United Kingdom, 2007).

[42]Government of Canada, *From Impacts to Adaptation: Canada in a Changing Climate 2007* (Ottawa, Ontario, 2008).

[43]Australian Government Department of Climate Change, *Climate Change Adaptation Actions for Local Government* (Canberra, Australia, 2009).

had been completed as of October 2008. The NAPAs communicate the country's priority activities addressing the urgent and immediate needs and concerns relating to adaptation to the adverse effects of climate change.

In order to provide an in-depth example of a climate change adaptation effort outside of the United States, we selected the United Kingdom as a case study to better understand some of the actions that government officials can take to adapt to climate change. We selected the United Kingdom because it has initiated a coordinated climate change adaptation response at the national, regional, and local levels.

Over the past decade, the issuance of prominent reports and the fallout from major weather events created awareness among government officials of the need for the United Kingdom to adapt to inevitable changes to the nation's climate. For example, in 2002, the London Climate Change Partnership, a stakeholder-led group coordinated by the Greater London Authority, issued a report called *London's Warming*, which detailed the expected impacts of climate change and the key challenges to addressing it.[44] In addition, the 2006 *Stern Review* of the economics of climate change helped accelerate the national government's efforts to adapt.[45] These and other reports show that the United Kingdom could experience a variety of climate change effects in the future, including dry summers, wet winters, coastal erosion, and sea level rise.

In fact, the United Kingdom is already experiencing severe weather events. For example, in 2006, a dry period brought about water restrictions in London. The following year, large-scale flooding in the United Kingdom highlighted the need to respond to climate change and led to the *Pitt Review*, which examined resilience to flooding in the United Kingdom.[46] In addition, the nation's insurance sector, which currently offers comprehensive flood insurance coverage, has raised concerns about the growing flood risk and asked for government action.

---

[44]London Climate Change Partnership. *London's Warming: The Impacts of Climate Change on London* (London, United Kingdom, November 2002).

[45]Nicholas Stern, *Stern Review: The Economics of Climate Change* (October 2006).

[46]Michael Pitt, *Pitt Review: Learning Lessons from the 2007 Floods* (June 2008).

In response to these concerns, the United Kingdom enacted national climate change legislation in 2008.[47] The law requires the British Secretary of State for Environment, Food and Rural Affairs to report periodically to Parliament with a risk assessment of the current and predicted impacts of climate change and to propose programs and policies for climate change adaptation. The law also authorizes the national government to require certain public authorities, such as water companies, to report on their assessment of the current and predicted impact of climate change in relation to the authority's functions as well as their proposals and policies for adapting to climate change. According to Department for Environment, Food and Rural Affairs (DEFRA) officials, the government department responsible for leading action on adaptation, an independent expert subcommittee of the Committee on Climate Change is to provide technical advice and oversee these efforts. The United Kingdom is also working with the European Union to incorporate climate change into its decisions and policies.

In the United Kingdom, different levels of government report working together to ensure that climate change considerations are incorporated into decision making. For example, the Government Office for London chairs the national government's Local and Regional Adaptation Partnership Board, which aims to facilitate climate change adaptation at local and regional levels by highlighting best practices and encouraging information sharing among local and regional officials. According to DEFRA officials, the primary role of the national government is to provide information, raise awareness, and encourage others to take action, not dictate how to adapt. In response to the United Kingdom's 2008 Climate Change Act, DEFRA officials said they are preparing a national risk assessment and conducting economic analyses to quantify the costs and benefits of adaptive actions. DEFRA officials said that these steps are to assist adaptation efforts undertaken by the national government, local government officials, and the private sector.

Adaptation activities are driven in part by the use of national performance measures, which affect local funding, and national government programs, according to DEFRA officials. The national government recently introduced a national adaptation indicator, which measures how well local governments are adapting to climate change risk. Performance measured by this and other indicators is the basis for national grants to local

---

[47]Climate Change Act 2008, ch. 27 (Eng.).

governments. Individual government agencies are also developing and implementing their own plans to address climate change effects. For example, the Environment Agency, which is responsible for environmental protection in England and Wales, as well as flood defense and water resource management, has initiatives in place to reduce water use to increase resilience to drought. It is also addressing flood risk, most notably with the Thames Barrier, a series of flood gates that protect London from North Sea storms (see fig. 6).

The Thames Barrier is a flood control system designed by the Greater London Council to respond to severe floods in 1953. The Thames Estuary 2100 plan, which was released for public comment on March 31, 2009, was undertaken to determine whether London's flood control infrastructure, including the Thames Barrier, can continue to protect London given the projections for sea level rise and expected development. The Environment Agency, which operates the barrier, relied on models of sea level rise to determine that continuation of current operations with some marginal improve-ments, such as using the barrier's gates' ability to "over-rotate," combined with other measures throughout the floodplain, would be sufficient at this time. The plan includes a monitoring component and a schedule to take further action later this century.

Figure 6: The Thames Barrier, London, United Kingdom

Bottom: Thames Barrier piers (the gates are underwater between the piers); top: a Thames Barrier gate rotated out of the water.

Source: GAO.

The United Kingdom's climate change initiatives are built around locally relevant information generated centrally by two primary sources. The United Kingdom Climate Impacts Programme (UKCIP), a primarily publicly funded program housed in Oxford University, generates stakeholder-centered climate change decision-making tools and facilitates responses to climate change. UKCIP works with national, regional, and local users of climate data to increase awareness and encourage actions. For example, Hampshire County, in southern England, used climate scenarios generated by UKCIP to complete a test of the county's sensitivity to weather and other emergency scenarios. The Met Office Hadley Centre, a government-funded climate research center, generates climate science information and develops models. According to a United

Kingdom official, the Met Office Hadley Centre generated the bulk of the science for the UK Climate Projections 2009, while UKCIP, among others, provided user guidance and training to facilitate the use of these data.[48]

Regional and international partnerships have also played a significant role in providing guidance to further climate change adaptation efforts in the United Kingdom. For example, Government Office for London officials told us that the Three Regions Climate Change Group (which includes the East of England, South East of England, and London) has set up a group to promote retrofitting of existing homes. The group produced a report, which provided a checklist for developers, case studies, a good practices guide, and a breakdown of the costs involved.[49] On an international scale, Greater London Authority officials stated that they are working with cities such as Tokyo, Toronto, and New York City to share knowledge about climate change adaptation. In addition, a Hampshire County Council official told us about the county's participation in the European Spatial Planning—Adapting to Climate Events project, which provided policy guidance and decision-making tools to governments from several countries on incorporating adaptation into planning decisions.

Federal, State, and Local Officials Face Numerous Challenges When Considering Climate Change Adaptation Efforts

The challenges faced by federal, state, and local officials in their efforts to adapt fell into three categories, based on our analysis of questionnaire results, site visits, and available studies. First, available attention and resources are focused on more immediate needs, making it difficult for adaptation efforts to compete for limited funds. Second, insufficient site-specific data, such as local projections of expected changes, makes it hard to predict the impacts of climate change, and thus hard for officials to justify the current costs of adaptation efforts for potentially less certain future benefits. Third, adaptation efforts are constrained by a lack of clear roles and responsibilities among federal, state, and local agencies.

---

[48]The UK Climate Projections (UKCP09) provide climate information for the United Kingdom up to the end of this century. See http://ukcp09.defra.gov.uk/.

[49]*Your Home in a Changing Climate: Retrofitting Existing Homes for Climate Change Impacts*, a special report prepared at the request of the Three Regions Climate Change Group, February 2008.

Competing Priorities Make It Difficult to Use Limited Funds on Adaptation Efforts

Competing priorities limit the ability of officials to respond to the impacts of climate change, based on our analysis of Web-based questionnaire results, site visits, and available studies. We asked federal, state, and local officials to rate specific challenges related to awareness and priorities as part of our questionnaire. Table 2 presents the percentage of federal, state, and local respondents who rated these challenges as very or extremely challenging in our questionnaire. Appendix III includes a more detailed summary of federal, state, and local officials' responses to the questionnaire.

Table 2: Percentage of Challenges Related to Awareness and Priorities Rated as Very or Extremely Challenging

How challenging are each of the following for officials when considering climate change adaptation efforts?	Total responses[a]	Percentage who rated as very or extremely challenging[b]
Lack of funding for adaptation efforts	179	83.8
Non-adaptation activities are higher priorities	180	71.1
Lack of clear priorities for allocating resources for adaptation activities	181	70.2
Lack of public awareness or knowledge of adaptation	184	61.4
Lack of a specific mandate to address climate change adaptation	182	57.7
Lack of awareness or knowledge of adaptation among government officials	182	57.7
Lack of clarity about what activities are considered adaptation	181	55.2
Difficult to define adaptation goals and performance metrics	181	55.8
Lack of qualified staff to work on adaptation efforts	181	50.3

Source: GAO.

[a]The total column represents the number of officials who answered each question using numerical ratings, ranging from (1) not at all challenging through (5) extremely challenging, out of the 187 respondents that completed the questionnaire.

[b]The percentage column represents the number of officials rating each challenge as (4) very challenging or (5) extremely challenging divided by the total number of numerical ratings submitted by officials for (1) not at all challenging through (5) extremely challenging.

The highest rated challenge identified by respondents was an overall lack of funding for adaptation efforts. This problem is coupled with the competing priorities of more immediate concerns.

Lack of funding: The government officials who responded to our questionnaire identified the lack of funding for adaptation efforts as both the top challenge related to awareness and priorities and the top overall challenge explored in our questionnaire. Several respondents wrote that lack of funding limited their ability to identify and respond to the impacts of climate change, with one noting, for example, that "we have the tools, but we just need the funding and leadership to act." A state official similarly said that "we need a large and dedicated funding source for adaptation. It's going to take 5 to 10 years of funding to get a body of information that will help planning in the long run. We need to start doing that planning and research now." Several studies also suggested that it will be difficult, if not impossible, for any agency to approach the tasks associated with adaptation without permanent, dedicated funding. For example, a recent federal report on adaptation options for climate-sensitive ecosystems and resources stated that a lack of sufficient resources may pose a significant barrier to adaptation efforts.[50]

Officials also cited lack of funding as a challenge during our site visits. For example, King County officials said that they do not have resources budgeted directly for addressing climate change. Instead, the county tries to meet its adaptation goals by shifting staff and reprioritizing goals. The county officials said it was difficult to take action without dedicated funding because some adaptation options are perceived to be very expensive, and that if available funding cannot support the consideration of adaptation options then the old ways of doing business would remain the norm.

Competing priorities: Respondents' concerns over an overall lack of funding for adaptation efforts was further substantiated, and perhaps explained, by their ratings of challenges related to the priority of adaptation relative to other concerns. Specifically, about 71 percent (128 of 180) of the respondents rated the challenge "non-adaptation activities are higher priorities" as very or extremely challenging. The responses of federal, state, and local respondents differed for this challenge. Specifically, about 79 percent (37 of 47) of state officials and nearly 76 percent (44 of 58) of local officials who responded to the question rated "non-adaptation activities are higher priorities" as very or extremely challenging, compared with about 61 percent (44 of 72) of the responding federal officials.[51]

---

[50]S.H. Julius, J.M. West (eds.), J.S. Baron, B. Griffith, L.A. Joyce, P. Kareiva, B.D. Keller, M.A. Palmer, C.H. Peterson, and J.M. Scott, *Preliminary Review of Adaptation Options for Climate-Sensitive Ecosystems and Resources*, Final Report, SAP 4.4.

[51]Differences by level of government (federal, state, and local) that are reported are for illustrative purposes and may not be statistically different. We present selected examples where the difference between federal, state, or local responses is greater than 15 percent and the difference presents useful context for the overall results. There were other differences by level of government that are not presented in this report.

Several federal, state, and local officials noted in their narrative comments in our questionnaire how difficult it is to convince managers of the need to plan for long-term adaptation when they are responsible for more urgent concerns that have short-term decision-making time frames. One federal official explained that "it all comes down to resource prioritization. Election and budget cycles complicate long-term planning such as adaptation will require. Without clear top-down leadership setting this as a priority, projects with benefits beyond the budget cycle tend to get raided to pay current-year bills to deliver results in this political cycle." Several other officials who responded to our questionnaire expressed similar sentiments. A recent NRC report similarly concluded that, in some cases, decision makers do not prioritize adaptation because they do not recognize the link to climate change in the day-to-day decisions that they make.[52]

Our August 2007 report on climate change on federal lands shows how climate change impacts compete for the attention of decision makers with more immediate priorities.[53] This report found that resource management agencies did not, at that time, make climate change a priority, nor did their agencies' strategic plans specifically address climate change. Resource managers explained that they had a wide range of responsibilities and that without their management designating climate change as a priority, they focused first on near-term priorities.

Our questionnaire results and site visits demonstrate that public awareness can play an important role in the prioritization of adaptation efforts. About 61 percent (113 of 184) of the officials who responded to our questionnaire rated "lack of public awareness or knowledge of adaptation" as either very or extremely challenging. The need to adapt to climate change is a complicated issue to communicate with the public because the impacts vary by location and may occur well into the future. For example, officials in Maryland told us that, while the public may be aware that climate change will affect the polar ice cap, people do not realize that it will also affect Maryland. New York City officials said that it is easier to engage the public once climate change effects are translated

---

[52]National Research Council of the National Academies, Panel on Strategies and Methods for Climate-Related Decision Support, Committee on the Human Dimensions of Global Change, *Informing Decisions in a Changing Climate*.

[53]GAO, *Climate Change: Agencies Should Develop Guidance for Addressing the Effects on Federal Land and Water Resources*, GAO-07-863 (Washington, D.C.: Aug. 7, 2007).

GAO-10-113 Climate Change Adaptation

into specific concerns, such as subway flooding. They said the term climate change adaptation can seem too abstract to the public.

Lack of Site-Specific Information Limits Adaptation Efforts

As summarized in table 3 and corroborated by our site visits and available studies, a lack of site-specific information—including information about the future benefits of adaptation activities—limits the ability of officials to respond to the impacts of climate change. See appendix III for a more detailed summary of federal, state, and local officials' responses to our Web-based questionnaire.

Table 3: Percentage of Challenges Related to Information Rated as Very or Extremely Challenging

How challenging are each of the following for officials when considering climate change adaptation efforts?	Total responses[a]	Percentage who rated as very or extremely challenging[b]
Justifying the current costs of adaptation efforts for potentially less certain future benefits	179	79.3
Size and complexity of *future* climate change impacts	180	76.7
Translating available climate information (e.g., projected temperature, precipitation) into impacts at the local level (e.g., increased stream flow)	182	74.7
Availability of climate information at relevant scale (i.e., downscaled regional and local information)	179	74.3
Understanding the costs and benefits of adaptation efforts	180	70
Lack of information about thresholds (i.e., limits beyond which recovery is impossible or difficult)	175	64.6
Making management and policy decisions with uncertainty about future effects of climate change	184	64.1
Lack of baseline monitoring data to enable evaluation of adaptation actions (i.e., inability to detect change)	181	62.4
Lack of certainty about the timing of climate change impacts	180	57.2
Accessibility and usability of available information on climate impacts and adaptation	182	53.3
Size and complexity of *current* climate change impacts	179	48.6

Source: GAO.

[a]The total column represents the number of officials who answered each question using numerical ratings, ranging from (1) not at all challenging through (5) extremely challenging, out of the 187 respondents that completed the questionnaire.

[b]The percentage column represents the number of officials rating each challenge as (4) very challenging or (5) extremely challenging divided by the total number of numerical ratings submitted by officials for (1) not at all challenging through (5) extremely challenging.

These challenges generally fit into two main categories: (1) the difficulty in justifying the current costs of adaptation with limited information about future benefits and (2) translating climate data—such as projected temperature and precipitation changes—into information that officials need to make decisions.

Justifying current costs with limited information about future benefits:
Respondents rated "justifying the current costs of adaptation efforts for potentially less certain future benefits" as the greatest challenge related to information and as the second greatest of all the challenges we asked about. They rated the "size and complexity of future climate change impacts" as the second greatest challenge related to information.[54] These concerns are not new. In fact, a 1993 report on climate change adaptation by the Congressional Office of Technology Assessment posed the following question within its overall discussion of the issue: "why adopt a policy today to adapt to a climate change effect that may not occur, for which there is significant uncertainty about impacts, and for which benefits of the anticipatory measure may not be seen for decades?"[55] Several officials shared similar reactions in written responses to our questionnaire. For example, one local official asked, "How do we justify added expenses in a period of limited resources when the benefits are not clear?"

While the costs of policies to mitigate and adapt to climate change may be considerable, it is difficult to estimate the costs of inaction—costs which could be much greater, according to a recent NRC report.[56] This report cites the long time horizon associated with climate change, coupled with deep uncertainties associated with forecasts and projections, among other issues, as aspects of climate change that are challenging for decision making. Several officials who responded to our questionnaire noted similar concerns. For example, one federal official stated that decision makers needed to confront "the reality that the future will not echo the past and that we will forever be managing under future uncertainty."

---

[54]About 77 percent of the officials who responded to our questionnaire rated the "size and complexity of *future* climate change impacts" as very or extremely challenging, whereas only about 49 percent of the officials rated the "size and complexity of *current* climate change impacts" similarly.

[55]While noting that it may be appealing to delay adaptation actions given uncertainty associated with where, when, and how much change will occur, the report also states that delay may leave the nation poorly prepared to deal with the changes that do occur and may increase the possibility of impacts that are irreversible or otherwise very costly. See U.S. Congress, Office of Technology Assessment, *Preparing for an Uncertain Climate—Volume I*, OTA-O-567 (Washington, D.C.: U.S. Government Printing Office, October 1993).

[56]National Research Council of the National Academies, Panel on Strategies and Methods for Climate-Related Decision Support, Committee on the Human Dimensions of Global Change, *Informing Decisions in a Changing Climate.*

Of particular importance in adaptation are planning decisions involving physical infrastructure projects, which require large capital investments and which, by virtue of their anticipated lifespan, will have to be resilient to changes in climate for many decades.[57] The long lead time and long life of large infrastructure investments require such decisions to be made well before climate change effects are discernable. For example, the United Kingdom Environment Agency's Thames 2100 Plan, which was released for consultation in April 2009, maps out necessary maintenance and operations needs for the Thames Barrier until 2070, at which point major changes will be required. Since constructing flood gates is a long-term process (the current barrier was finished 30 years after officials first identified a need for it), officials said they need the information now, even if the threat will not materialize until later.

Translating climate data into site-specific information: The process of providing useful information to officials making decisions about adaptation can be summarized in several steps.

First, data from global-scale models must be "downscaled" to provide climate information at a geographic scale relevant to decision makers. About 74 percent (133 of 179) of the officials who responded to our questionnaire rated "availability of climate information at relevant scale (i.e., downscaled regional and local information)" as very or extremely challenging. In addition, according to one federal respondent, "until we better understand what the impacts of climate change will be at spatial (and temporal) scales below what the General Circulation Models predict for the global scale, it will be difficult to identify specific adaptation strategies that respond to specific impacts."[58]

Our August 2007 report on climate change on federal lands demonstrated that resource managers did not have sufficient site-specific information to plan for and manage the effects of climate change on the federal resources

---

[57]Government of Canada, *From Impacts to Adaptation: Canada in a Changing Climate 2007* (Ottawa, Ontario, 2008).

[58]A General Circulation Model (GCM) is a global, three-dimensional computer model of the climate system which can be used to simulate human-induced climate change. GCMs are highly complex and they represent the effects of such factors as reflective and absorptive properties of atmospheric water vapor, greenhouse gas concentrations, clouds, annual and daily solar heating, ocean temperatures, and ice boundaries. The most recent GCMs include global representations of the atmosphere, oceans, and land surface.

they oversee.[59] In particular, the managers lacked computational models for local projections of expected changes. For example, at that time, officials at the Florida Keys National Marine Sanctuary said that they lacked adequate modeling and scientific information to enable managers to predict change on a small scale, such as that occurring within the sanctuary. Without such models, the managers' options were limited to reacting to already-observed effects.

Second, climate information must be translated into impacts at the local level, such as increased stream flow. About 75 percent (136 of 182) of the respondents rated "translating available climate information (e.g., projected temperature, precipitation) into impacts at the local level (e.g., increased stream flow)" as very or extremely challenging. Some respondents and officials interviewed during our site visits said that it is challenging to link predicted temperature and precipitation changes to specific impacts. For example, one federal respondent said that "we often lack fundamental information on how ecological systems/species respond to non-climate change related anthropogenic stresses, let alone how they will respond to climate change." Such predictions may not easily or directly match the information needs that could inform management decisions. For example, Maryland officials told us they do not have information linking climate model information, such as temperature and precipitation changes, to biological impacts, such as changes to tidal marshes. Similarly, King County officials said they are not sure how to translate climate change information into effects on salmon recovery efforts. Specifically, they said that there is incomplete information about how climate change may affect stream temperatures, stream flows, and other factors important to salmon recovery.

However, multiple respondents said that it was not necessary to have specific, detailed, downscaled modeling to manage for adaptation in the short term. For example, one federal respondent said that although modeling projections will get better over time, there will always be elements of uncertainty in how systems and species will react to climate change. Interestingly, federal, state, and local respondents perceived the challenges posed by site-specific information needs differently. About 85 percent (60 of 71) of the federal officials that responded to the question rated "translating available climate information into impacts at the local level" as very or extremely challenging, compared to around 75 percent

---

[59]GAO-07-863.

(35 of 47) of the state officials and around 66 percent (40 of 59) of the local officials who responded.

Third, local impacts must be translated into costs and benefits, since this information is required for many decision-making processes. Almost 70 percent (126 of 180) of the respondents to our questionnaire rated "understanding the costs and benefits of adaptation efforts" as very or extremely challenging. As noted by one local government respondent, it is important to understand the costs and benefits of adaptation efforts so they can be evaluated relative to other priorities. In addition, a federal respondent said that tradeoffs between costs and benefits are an important component to making decisions under uncertainty.

Fourth, decision makers need baseline monitoring data to evaluate adaptation actions over time. Nearly 62 percent (113 of 181) of the respondents to our questionnaire rated the "lack of baseline monitoring data to enable evaluation of adaptation actions (i.e., inability to detect change)" as very or extremely challenging, one of the lower ratings for this category of challenges. As summarized by a recent NRC report, officials will need site-specific and relevant baselines of environmental, social, and economic information against which past and current decisions can be monitored, assessed, and changed.[60] Future decision-making success will be judged on how quickly and effectively numerous ongoing decisions can be adjusted to changing circumstances. For example, according to Maryland officials, the state lacks baseline data on certain key Chesapeake Bay species such as blue crab and striped bass, so it will be difficult to determine how climate change will affect them or if proposed adaptation measures were successful. Similarly, our August 2007 report on climate change on federal lands showed that resource managers generally lacked detailed inventories and monitoring systems to provide them with an adequate baseline understanding of the plant and animal species that existed on the resources they manage.[61] Without such information, it was difficult for managers to determine whether observed changes were within the normal range of variability.

---

[60]National Research Council of the National Academies, Panel on Strategies and Methods for Climate-Related Decision Support, Committee on the Human Dimensions of Global Change, *Informing Decisions in a Changing Climate*.

[61]GAO-07-863.

Adaptation Efforts Are Constrained by a Lack of Clear Roles and Responsibilities

A lack of clear roles and responsibilities for addressing adaptation across all levels of government limits adaptation efforts, based on our analysis of federal, state, and local officials' responses to our Web-based questionnaire, site visits, and relevant studies. Table 4 presents respondents' views on how challenging different aspects of the structure and operation of the federal government are to adaptation efforts. See appendix III for a more detailed summary of federal, state, and local officials' responses to our Web-based questionnaire.

Table 4: Percentage of Challenges Related to the Structure and Operation of the Federal Government Rated as Very or Extremely Challenging

How challenging are each of the following for officials when considering climate change adaptation efforts?	Total responses[a]	Percentage who rated as very or extremely challenging[b]
Lack of clear roles and responsibilities for addressing adaptation across all levels of government (i.e., adaptation is everyone's problem but nobody's direct responsibility)	178	69.7
The authority and capability to adapt is spread among many federal agencies (i.e., institutional fragmentation)	176	58
Lack of federal guidance or policies on how to make decisions related to adaptation	176	52.3
Existing federal policies, programs, or practices that hinder adaptation efforts	150	42.7
Federal statutory, regulatory, or other legal constraints on adaptation efforts	152	36.2

Source: GAO.

[a]The total column represents the number of officials who answered each question using numerical ratings, ranging from (1) not at all challenging through (5) extremely challenging, out of the 187 respondents that completed the questionnaire.

[b]The percentage column represents the number of officials rating each challenge as (4) very challenging or (5) extremely challenging divided by the total number of numerical ratings submitted by officials for (1) not at all challenging through (5) extremely challenging.

These challenges are summarized in two general categories: (1) lack of clear roles and responsibilities and (2) federal activities that constrain adaptation efforts.

Lack of clear roles and responsibilities: "A lack of clear roles and responsibilities for addressing adaptation across all levels of government (i.e., adaptation is everyone's problem but nobody's direct responsibility)" was identified by respondents as the greatest challenge related to the structure and operation of the federal government. Several respondents elaborated on their rating. For example, according to one state official, "there is a power struggle between agencies and levels of government rather than a lack of clear roles. Everyone wants to take the lead rather than working together in a collaborative and cohesive way." One local official said he "can't emphasize enough how the lack of coordination between agencies at the federal (and state) level severely complicates our abilities at the local level." Several respondents also noted that there is no element within the federal government charged with facilitating a collaborative response. Our questionnaire results show that local and state respondents consider the lack of clear roles and responsibilities to be a greater challenge than do federal respondents. Specifically, about 80 percent (48 of 60) of local officials and about 67 percent (31 of 46) of state officials who responded to the question rated the lack of clear roles and responsibilities as either very or extremely challenging, compared with about 61 percent (42 of 69) of the responding federal officials.

This lack of coordination and "institutional fragmentation" are serious challenges to adaptation efforts because clear roles are necessary for a large-scale response to climate change. As stated by one local government respondent, agencies "have numerous, overlapping jurisdictions and authorities, many of which have different (sometimes competing) mandates. If left to plan independently, they'll either do no adaptation planning or, if they do, likely come up with very different (and potentially conflicting) adaptation priorities." A recent NRC report comes to similar conclusions, noting that collaboration among agencies can be impeded by different enabling laws, opposing missions, or incompatible budgetary rules.[62] Such barriers—whether formalized or implicit—can lead to disconnects, conflicts, and turf battles rather than productive cooperation, according to this report.

About 52 percent (92 of 176) of the respondents to our questionnaire rated the "lack of federal guidance or policies on how to make decisions related to adaptation" as very or extremely challenging. Their views echo our August 2007 report, which noted that federal resource managers were constrained by limited guidance about whether or how to address climate change and, therefore, were uncertain about what actions, if any, they should take.[63] In general, resource managers from all of the agencies we reviewed for that report said that they needed specific guidance to incorporate climate change into their management actions and planning efforts. For example, officials from several federal land and water resource management agencies said that guidance would help resolve

---

[62]National Research Council of the National Academies, Panel on Strategies and Methods for Climate-Related Decision Support, Committee on the Human Dimensions of Global Change, *Informing Decisions in a Changing Climate*.

[63]GAO-07-863.

differences in their agencies about how to interpret broad resource management authorities with respect to climate change and give them an imperative to take action.

A recent federal report on adaptation options for climate-sensitive ecosystems and resources reinforced these points.[64] It noted that, as resource managers become aware of climate change and the challenges it poses, a major limitation is lack of guidance on what steps to take, especially guidance that is commensurate with agency cultures and the practical experiences that managers have accumulated from years of dealing with other stresses, such as droughts and fires.

Our questionnaire results indicate that local government respondents consider the lack of federal guidance to be a greater challenge than state or federal respondents. Specifically, about 65 percent (39 of 60) of local officials who responded to the question rated the "lack of federal guidance or policies on how to make decisions related to adaptation" as either very or extremely challenging, compared to about 41 percent (19 of 46) of state officials and nearly 49 percent (33 of 67) of the federal officials that responded.

Federal activities that constrain adaptation efforts: Another challenge related to the structure and operation of the federal government is the existence of federal policies, programs, or practices that hinder adaptation efforts. While not the top challenge in the category, "existing federal policies, programs, or practices that hinder adaptation efforts"—which was rated as very or extremely challenging by about 43 percent (64 of 150) of the officials who responded to our questionnaire—is an important issue, as indicated by a wealth of related written comments submitted by respondents, comments from officials at our site visits, and a number of related studies.

Our work shows how, at least in some instances, federal programs may limit adaptation efforts. Our 2007 climate change-related report on FEMA's National Flood Insurance Program and the U.S. Department of Agriculture's (USDA) Federal Crop Insurance Corporation, which insures crops against drought or other weather disasters, contrasted the

---

[64]Julius, S.H., J.M. West (eds.), J.S. Baron, B. Griffith, L.A. Joyce, P. Kareiva, B.D. Keller, M.A. Palmer, C.H. Peterson, and J.M. Scott, *Preliminary Review of Adaptation Options for Climate-Sensitive Ecosystems and Resources*, Final Report, SAP 4.4.

experience of public and private insurers.[65] We found that many major private insurers were incorporating some near-term elements of climate change into their risk management practices. In addition, we found that some private insurers were approaching climate change at a strategic level by publishing reports outlining the potential industrywide impacts and strategies to proactively address the issue. In contrast, our report noted that the agencies responsible for the nation's key federal insurance programs had done little to develop the kind of information needed to understand their programs' long-term exposure to climate change for a variety of reasons. As a FEMA official explained in that report, the National Flood Insurance Program is designed to assess and insure against current—not future—risks. Unlike the private sector, neither this program nor the Federal Crop Insurance Corporation had analyzed the potential impacts of an increase in the frequency or severity of weather-related events on their operations. At our site visit, Maryland officials told us that FEMA's outdated delineation of floodplains, as well as its failure to consider changes in floodplain boundaries due to sea level rise, is allowing development in areas that are vulnerable to sea level rise in Maryland because local governments rely on its maps for planning purposes. Both FEMA and USDA have taken recent steps to address these concerns and have committed to study these issues further and report to Congress, with USDA estimating completion by December 31, 2009.[66]

Officials who responded to our questionnaire also identified several federal laws that hinder climate change efforts. A state official noted that many federal laws such as the Endangered Species Act, the Clean Water Act, and the Clean Air Act were passed before recognition of the effects of climate change. A federal official stated that federal environmental laws may need to be amended to provide greater authority for agencies to

---

[65]GAO-07-285.

[66]As mentioned, FEMA is currently conducting a study on the impact of climate change on the National Flood Insurance Program, which will be completed in March 2010. According to FEMA, this study will provide policy options and recommendations regarding the effects of climate change on the National Flood Insurance Program. At USDA, the Risk Management Agency has contracted with a research group to provide a technical report on climate change impacts on the Federal Crop Insurance Corporation and develop a program impact model. The contractor has submitted preliminary results and the final report is due by December of this year. Using information contained in the report and other information, the Risk Management Agency will evaluate how it can adapt the crop insurance program to accommodate potential climate change scenarios.

practice adaptive management.[67] The official noted that federal laws promoting development may also warrant re-examination to the extent they provide incentives that run counter to prudent land and resource planning in the climate change context.

One federal respondent stated that federal laws, regulations, and policies assume that long-term climate is stable and that species, ecosystems, and water resources can be managed to maintain the status quo or to restore them to prior conditions. This official observed that these objectives may no longer be achievable as climate change intensifies in the coming decades. A state official similarly noted that because of the effects of climate change, maintenance of the resource management status quo in any given area may no longer be possible. Part of the problem may lie in the inherent tension between the order of legal frameworks and the relative chaos of natural systems, which one legal commentator explained as follows: "Lawyers like rules. We like enforceable rules. We want our rules to be optimal, tidy, and timeless…. Collaborative ecosystem management, by contrast, is often messy, elaborate, cumbersome, ad hoc, and defiantly unconventional."[68] Several officials who responded to our questionnaire expressed similar concerns related to climate change adaptation. For example, one federal official stated that existing laws "were built for the status quo, but we now must re-engineer the entire legal framework to deal with the ongoing, perpetual, and rapid change. A systems view is essential in order to manage change optimally."

---

[67]In 2004, NRC defined adaptive management as a process that promotes flexible decision making in the face of uncertainties, as outcomes from management actions and other events become better understood. See GAO, *Yellowstone Bison: Interagency Plan and Agencies' Management Need Improvement to Better Address Bison-Cattle Brucellosis Controversy*, GAO-08-291 (Washington, D.C.: Mar. 7, 2008). Adaptive management can be used to reduce the adverse effects of climate change on ecosystems. See C. Parmesan and H. Galbraith, *Observed Impacts of Global Climate Change in the U.S.* (2004). However, significant challenges confront those wishing to apply the technique to complex problems, such as addressing the effects of climate change on land use designations in land management plans prepared under the National Forest Management Act or the Federal Land Policy and Management Act of 1976. See R. Gregory et. al., "Deconstructing Adaptive Management: Criteria for Applications to Environmental Management," *Ecological Applications*, vol. 16, no. 6 (December 2006). Indeed, adaptive management "may be most difficult to implement in precisely those circumstances in which it is most needed." *Id.*

[68]Karkkainen, "Collaborative Ecosystem Governance: Scale, Complexity, and Dynamism," 21 *Va. Envtl. L.J.* 189, (2008): 243-35. Karkkainen's advice to lawyers who are unsettled by this apparent conflict is "let's get over it." *Id.* at 235.

Federal Efforts to Increase Awareness, Provide Relevant Information, and Define Responsibilities Could Help Government Officials Make Decisions about Adaptation

Potential federal actions for addressing challenges to adaptation efforts fall into three areas, based on our analysis of questionnaire results, site visits, and available studies: (1) federal training and education initiatives that could increase awareness among government officials and the public about the impacts of climate change and available adaptation strategies; (2) actions to provide and interpret site-specific information that could help officials understand the impacts of climate change at a scale that would enable them to respond; and (3) steps Congress and federal agencies could take to encourage adaptation by setting priorities and re-evaluating programs that hinder adaptation efforts.

Federal Training and Education Initiatives Would Assist Adaptation Efforts

Federal training and education initiatives would assist adaptation efforts, based on our analysis of our Web-based questionnaire, site visits, and relevant studies. Table 5 presents potential federal government actions related to awareness and priorities as rated by federal, state, and local officials who responded to our questionnaire. See appendix III for a more detailed summary of federal, state, and local officials' responses to our Web-based questionnaire.

Table 5: Percentage of Potential Federal Government Actions Related to Awareness and Priorities Rated as Very or Extremely Useful

How useful, if at all, would each of the following federal government actions be for officials in efforts to adapt to a changing climate?	Total responses[a]	Percentage who rated as very or extremely useful[b]
Development of regional or local educational workshops for relevant officials that are tailored to their responsibilities	182	74.7
Development of lists of "no regrets" actions (i.e., actions in which the benefits exceed the costs under all future climate scenarios)	181	73.5
Development of a list of potential climate change adaptation policy options	181	71.3
Creation of a campaign to educate the public about climate change adaptation	184	70.1
Training of relevant officials on adaptation issues	182	69.8
Creation of a recurring stakeholder forum to explore the interaction of climate science and adaptation practice	184	64.7
Prioritization of potential climate change adaptation options	183	61.7

Source: GAO.

[a]The total column represents the number of officials who answered each question using numerical ratings, ranging from (1) not at all useful through (5) extremely useful, out of the 187 respondents that completed the questionnaire.

[b]The percentage column represents the number of officials rating each potential action as (4) very useful or (5) extremely useful divided by the total numerical ratings submitted by officials for (1) not at all useful through (5) extremely useful.

We present these potential federal actions in three general categories: (1) training programs that could help government officials to develop more effective and better coordinated adaptation programs; (2) development of specific policy options for government officials; and (3) public education efforts to increase the public's understanding of climate change issues and the need to begin investing in preparatory measures.

Training for government officials: Training efforts could help officials collaborate and share insights for developing and implementing adaptation initiatives. Respondents rated the "development of regional or local educational workshops for relevant officials that are tailored to their responsibilities" as the most useful potential federal government action related to awareness and priorities. According to one federal official, "it is clear that training and communication may be the two biggest hurdles we face. We have the capabilities to adapt and to forecast scenarios of change and potential impacts of alternative adaptation options. We lack the will to exercise this capacity. The lack of that will is traceable to ignorance, sometimes willfully maintained." This respondent calls for "a massive educational process...designed and implemented all the way from the top-end strategic thinkers down to the ranks of tactical implementers of change and adaptation options." Training on how to make decisions with uncertainty would be particularly useful for frontline actors, such as city and county governments. For example, Maryland held an interactive summit on building "coast-smart communities," which brought together federal, state, and local officials involved with planning decisions in coastal areas. The summit employed role-playing to introduce participants to critical issues faced by coastal communities as a result of climate change. In addition, New York City DEP officials noted that their membership in the Water Utility Climate Alliance provided them with an important way to exchange information with water managers from across the nation.

Several respondents said that the federal government could play an important role in training officials at all levels of government. For example, one state official said that "because so many of us are only in the early stages of becoming aware of this issue, I think that a well organized training where many people would be learning the same thing and in the same way is important." However, a different state official questioned whether federal training would be effective for state and local officials, explaining that federal officials may not have enough knowledge about specific state and local challenges. The official thought that a better option may be to hold regional conferences with diverse groups of federal, state, and local officials so that those who are not up to speed can observe and learn from those who are. Interestingly, about 84 percent (38 of 45) of the state officials and nearly 75 percent (53 of 71) of the federal officials who responded to the question rated the "development of regional or local educational workshops for relevant officials that are tailored to their responsibilities" as very or extremely useful, compared to about 67 percent (42 of 63) of the local officials that responded.

Development of lists of policy options for government officials: The development of lists of "no regrets" actions—actions in which the benefits exceed the costs under all future climate scenarios—and other potential adaptation policy options could inform officials about efforts that make sense to pursue today and are "worth doing anyway." The Intergovernmental Panel on Climate Change defines a "no regrets" policy as one that would generate net social and economic benefits irrespective of whether or not anthropogenic climate change occurs. Such policies could include energy conservation and efficiency programs or the construction of green roofs in urban areas to absorb rainwater and moderate the effects of heat waves.

About 73 percent (133 of 181) of the officials who responded to our questionnaire rated the "development of lists of 'no regrets' actions (i.e., actions in which the benefits exceed the costs under all future climate scenarios)" as either very or extremely useful. The costs of no regrets strategies may be easier to defend, and proposing such strategies could be a way to initiate discussions of additional adaptation efforts. Likewise, about 71 percent (129 of 181) of respondents rated the "development of a list of potential climate change adaptation policy options" as either very or extremely useful.

However, several respondents questioned whether national lists of adaptation options would be useful, noting that adaptation is inherently local or regional in nature. For example, one federal official said that "it is unclear that it would be possible to develop a list of actions that truly is no regrets for all scenarios, all places, and all interested parties." This view suggests that adaptation options—"no regrets" or otherwise—may vary based on the climate impacts observed or projected for different geographic areas. As stated by one local official, "a national list would need to collect options from all regions across many sectors to be useful."

Regarding the prioritization of potential adaptation policy options, about 62 percent (113 of 183) of the respondents rated the "prioritization of potential climate change adaptation options" as very or extremely useful, the lowest-rated potential action related to awareness and priorities. Several respondents were adamant that prioritization should occur at the local level because of the variability of local impacts, and others said that federal agencies should assist such efforts, but not direct them. According to one state official respondent, federal efforts "should recognize and meet the needs of states and local governments. They should not…dictate policy." Interestingly, local officials who responded to our questionnaire rated prioritization of policy options as more useful than federal or state officials. Specifically, about 75 percent (47 of 63) of the local officials who responded to the question said that federal prioritization of potential climate change adaptation options would be very or extremely useful, compared to nearly 57 percent (40 of 70) and about 51 percent (24 of 47) of federal and state officials, respectively.

Public education: About 70 percent (129 of 184) of the respondents rated the "creation of a campaign to educate the public about climate change adaptation" as very or extremely useful. A variety of federal, state, and local programs are trying to fill this void, at least in areas of the country that are actively addressing adaptation issues. For example, the Chesapeake Bay National Estuarine Research Reserve (partially funded by

NOAA) provides education and training on climate change to the public and local officials in Maryland. Maryland state officials recently provided local officials and the public in Somerset County information on the effects of sea level rise during a workshop. The workshop highlighted the need to incorporate information about sea level rise in the county's land use plans, given that it is expected to inundate a significant part of the county. In addition, the University of Washington's Climate Impacts Group (CIG)—a program funded under NOAA's Regional Integrated Sciences and Assessment program—has been interacting with the public about climate change issues, including adaptation, for over 10 years, according to officials we interviewed as part of our site visit to King County, Washington. Considerable local media coverage of environmental issues has also assisted with public awareness in King County.

Federal Actions to Provide and Interpret Site-Specific Information Would Help Officials Implement Adaptation Efforts

Federal actions to provide and interpret site-specific information would help address challenges associated with adaptation efforts, based on our analysis of our Web-based questionnaire, site visits, and relevant studies. Table 6 presents potential federal government actions related to information as rated by federal, state, and local officials who responded to our questionnaire. See appendix III for a more detailed summary of federal, state, and local officials' responses to our Web-based questionnaire.

Table 6: Percentage of Potential Federal Government Actions Related to Information Rated as Very or Extremely Useful

How useful, if at all, would each of the following federal government actions be for officials in efforts to adapt to a changing climate?	Total responses[a]	Percentage who rated as very or extremely useful[b]
Development of *state and local* climate change impact and vulnerability assessments	183	80.3
Identification and sharing of best practices	157[c]	80.3
Development of processes and tools to help officials access, interpret, and apply available climate information	185	80.0
Development of *regional* climate change impact and vulnerability assessments	182	77.5
Creation of a federal service to consolidate and deliver climate information to decision makers to inform adaptation efforts	176	60.8
Development of an interactive stakeholder forum for information sharing	184	56.5

Source: GAO.

[a]The total column represents the number of officials who answered each question using numerical ratings, ranging from (1) not at all useful through (5) extremely useful, out of the 187 respondents that completed the questionnaire.

[b]The percentage column represents the number of officials rating each potential action as (4) very useful or (5) extremely useful divided by the total numerical ratings submitted by officials for (1) not at all useful through (5) extremely useful.

[c]As previously noted, 187 respondents completed our questionnaire overall. While the number of responses for each individual question generally ranged from 183 to 186, only 159 respondents answered this question. See appendix III for more details.

We discuss these potential federal actions below in three general categories: (1) the development of regional, state, and local climate change impact and vulnerability assessments; (2) the development of processes and tools to access, interpret, and apply climate information; and (3) the creation of a federal service to consolidate and deliver climate information to decision makers to inform adaptation efforts.

Developing impact and vulnerability assessments: Respondents rated the "development of state and local climate change impact and vulnerability assessments" as the most useful action the federal government could take related to information. The development of regional assessments was also rated as similarly useful by respondents. Such assessments allow officials to build adaptation strategies based on the best available knowledge about regional or local changes and how those changes may affect natural and human systems. Nearly 94 percent (43 of 46) of the state officials and about 83 percent (52 of 63) of the local officials who responded to the question rated the development of state and local climate change impact and vulnerability assessments as either very or extremely useful, compared to about 69 percent (49 of 71) of federal officials.

Officials at all of the sites we visited reported relying on impact and vulnerability assessments to drive policy development and focus on the most urgent adaptation needs. For example, King County officials told us that regional climate modeling information provided by CIG was used to conduct a vulnerability assessment of wastewater treatment facilities in the county. In addition, Maryland officials said that the state's coastal adaptation initiative relied on localized impact and vulnerability information provided by the Maryland Commission on Climate Change's Scientific and Technical Working Group, a stakeholder working group consisting of scientists and other relevant stakeholders.

Development of processes and tools to help officials use information: About 80 percent (148 of 185) of respondents rated the "development of processes and tools to help access, interpret, and apply available climate information" as very or extremely useful. Even with available regional and local climate data, officials will need tools to interpret what the data mean for decision making. For example, CIG told us of the strong need for Web-based decision-making tools to translate climate impacts into information relevant for decision makers. King County's Department of Natural Resources and Parks has developed a tool that uses data generated by CIG to help wastewater facilities model flooding due to sea level rise and storms. United Kingdom officials noted that the Climate Impacts Programme provides similar tools to assist decision makers in the United Kingdom.

The identification and sharing of best practices from other jurisdictions could also help meet the information needs of decision makers. Around 80 percent (126 of 157) of respondents rated the "identification and sharing of best practices" as very or extremely important. Best practices refer to the processes, practices, and systems identified in organizations that performed exceptionally well and are widely recognized as improving performance and efficiency in specific areas. Based on a range of our prior work, we have found that successfully identifying and applying best practices can reduce expenses and improve organizational efficiency. Several officials who responded to our questionnaire said that learning the best practices of others could be useful in efforts to develop adaptation programs.

Federal climate service: About 61 percent (107 of 176) of respondents rated the "creation of a federal service to consolidate and deliver climate information to decision makers to inform adaptation efforts" as very or extremely useful. According to two pending bills in Congress that would establish a National Climate Service within NOAA, its purpose would be to advance understanding of climate variability and change at the global, national, and regional levels and support the development of adaptation and response plans by federal agencies and state, local, and tribal governments.

Respondents offered a range of potential strengths and weaknesses for such a service. Several said that a National Climate Service would help consolidate information and provide a single-information resource for local officials, and others said that it would be an improvement over the current ad hoc system. A climate service would avoid duplication and establish an agreed set of climate information with uniform methodologies, benchmarks, and metrics for decision making, according to some officials. According to one federal official, consolidating scientific, modeling, and analytical expertise and capacity could increase efficiency. Some officials similarly noted that with such consolidation of information, individual agencies, states, and local governments would not have to spend money obtaining climate data for their adaptation efforts. Others said that it would be advantageous to work from one source of information instead of different sources of varying quality. Importantly, some officials said that a National Climate Service would demonstrate a federal commitment to adaptation and provide a credible voice and guidance to decision makers.

Other respondents, however, were less enthusiastic. Some voiced skepticism about whether it was feasible to consolidate climate information, and others said that such a system would be too rigid and may get bogged down in lengthy review processes. Furthermore, certain officials said building such capacity may not be the most effective place to focus federal efforts because the information needs of decision makers vary so much by jurisdiction. Several officials noted that climate change is an issue that requires a multidisciplinary response and a single federal service may not be able to supply all of the necessary expertise. For example, one federal official stated that the information needs of Bureau of Reclamation water managers are quite different from the needs of Bureau of Land Management rangeland managers, which are different from the needs of all other resource management agencies and programs. The official said that it seems highly unlikely that a single federal service could effectively identify and address the diverse needs of multiple agencies. Several respondents also said that having one preeminent source for climate change information and modeling could stifle contrary ideas and alternative viewpoints. Finally, several officials who responded to our questionnaire were concerned that a National Climate Service could divert attention and resources from current adaptation efforts by reinventing duplicative processes without making use of existing structures.

A recent NRC report recommends that the federal government's adaptation efforts should be undertaken through a new integrated interagency initiative with both service and research elements, but that such an initiative should not be centralized in a single agency.[69] Doing so, according to this report, would disrupt existing relationships between agencies and their constituencies and formalize a separation between the emerging science of climate response and fundamental research on climate and the associated biological, social, and economic phenomena. Furthermore, the report states that a National Climate Service located in a single agency and modeled on the weather service would by itself be less than fully effective for meeting the national needs for climate-related decision support. The NRC report also notes that such a climate service would not be user-driven and so would likely fall short in providing needed information, identifying and meeting critical needs for research for and on decision support, and adapting adequately to changing information needs.

Congress and Federal Agencies Could Encourage Adaptation Efforts by Clarifying Roles and Responsibilities

Federal actions to clarify the roles and responsibilities for government agencies could encourage adaptation efforts, based on our analysis of questionnaire results, site visits, and available studies. Table 7 presents potential federal actions related to the structure and operation of the federal government, as rated by the federal, state, and local officials who responded to our Web-based questionnaire. See appendix III for a more detailed summary of federal, state, and local officials' responses to our Web-based questionnaire.

---

[69]National Research Council of the National Academies, Panel on Strategies and Methods for Climate-Related Decision Support, Committee on the Human Dimensions of Global Change, *Informing Decisions in a Changing Climate.*

Table 7: Percentage of Potential Federal Government Actions Related to the Structure and Operation of the Federal Government Rated as Very or Extremely Useful

How useful, if at all, would each of the following federal government actions be for officials in efforts to adapt to a changing climate?	Total responses[a]	Percentage who rated as very or extremely useful[b]
Development of a national adaptation fund to provide a consistent funding stream for adaptation activities	179	84.4
Development of a national adaptation strategy that defines federal government priorities and responsibilities	181	71.3
Review of existing programs to identify and modify policies and practices that hinder adaptation efforts	180	67.8
Issuance of guidance, policies, or procedures on how to incorporate adaptation into existing policy and management processes	180	65.6
Development of a climate change extension service to help share and explain available information	181	59.1
Creation of a centralized government structure to coordinate adaptation funding	166	53.6

Source: GAO.

[a]The total column represents the number of officials who answered each question using numerical ratings, ranging from (1) not at all useful through (5) extremely useful, out of the 187 respondents that completed the questionnaire.

[b]The percentage column represents the number of officials rating each potential action as (4) very useful or (5) extremely useful divided by the total numerical ratings submitted by officials for (1) not at all useful through (5) extremely useful.

As discussed below, these potential federal actions can be grouped into three areas: (1) new national adaptation initiatives, (2) review of programs that hinder adaptation efforts, and (3) guidance for how to incorporate adaptation into existing decision-making processes.

New national adaptation initiatives: Our questionnaire results identified the "development of a national adaptation fund to provide a consistent funding stream for adaptation activities" as the most useful federal action related to the structure and operation of the federal government. This result is not surprising, given that lack of funding was identified as the greatest challenge to adaptation efforts. One local official said that "funding for local governments is absolutely required. Local budgets are tight and require external stimulus for any hope of adaptation strategies to be implemented." Several state respondents noted that none of the other potential policy options are maximally useful unless there is also consistent funding available to implement them. Overall, about 98 percent (45 of 46) of state officials and nearly 88 percent (56 of 64) of the local officials who responded to the question rated the development of a national adaptation fund to provide a consistent funding stream for adaptation activities as very or extremely useful, compared to about 71 percent (47 of 66) of federal officials.

About 71 percent (129 of 181) of the officials who responded to our questionnaire rated the "development of a national adaptation strategy that defines federal government priorities and responsibilities" as very or extremely useful. As noted by a federal official who responded to our questionnaire, the cost of responding to a changing climate will be paid one way or another—either through ad hoc responses to emergencies or through a coordinated effort at the federal level guided by the best foresight and planning afforded by the current science. According to this official, a strategic approach may cost less than reactive policies in the long term and could be more effective. Officials we spoke with at our site visits and officials who responded to our questionnaire said that a coordinated federal response would also demonstrate a federal commitment to adaptation.

About 59 percent (107 of 181) of respondents rated the "development of a climate change extension service to help share and explain available information" as very or extremely useful. A climate change extension service could operate in the same way as USDA's Cooperative State Research, Education, and Extension Service, with land grant universities and networks of local or regional offices staffed by experts providing useful, practical, and research-based information to agricultural producers, among others.[70] Such a service could be responsible for educating private citizens, city planners, and others at the local level whose responsibilities are climate sensitive. For example, Maryland Forest Service officials noted that the Maryland Cooperative Extension Service provides training and information on the significance of climate change. Several respondents cautioned that whatever is done at the federal level should be consistently and adequately funded.

About 54 percent (89 of 166) of respondents rated as very or extremely useful the "creation of a centralized government structure to coordinate adaptation funding." While some cautioned that such a structure could limit the flexibility of existing federal, state, and local programs, others said that there was a need for more coordinated funding. Support for the idea, however, varied by level of government. Specifically, about 73

---

[70]See http://www.csrees.usda.gov/Extension/ for more information about USDA's extension service.

GAO-10-113 Climate Change Adaptation

percent of the local (41 of 56) and almost 55 percent of the state (23 of 42) officials that responded to this question rated the "creation of a centralized federal government structure to coordinate adaptation funding" as either very or extremely useful, compared to only about 35 percent of the federal (23 of 65) respondents.

Reviewing programs that hinder adaptation: About 68 percent (122 of 180) of the respondents said it would be very or extremely useful to systematically review the kind of programs, policies, and practices discussed earlier in this report that may hinder adaptation efforts. Nearly 75 percent (46 of 61) of the local officials and about 70 percent (32 of 46) of the state officials who responded to the question rated the "review of existing programs to identify and modify policies and practices that hinder adaptation efforts" as very or extremely useful, compared to about 59 percent (41 of 70) of federal officials. One state official urged a review of both programs and laws, stating that "entrenched practices must be adapted to new realities." Our May 2008 report on the economics of climate change also identified actions that could assist officials in their efforts to adapt to climate change.[71] Some of the economists surveyed for that report suggested reforming insurance subsidy programs in areas vulnerable to natural disasters like hurricanes or flooding. Several noted that a clear federal role exists for certain sectors, such as water resource management, which could require additional resources for infrastructure development, research, and managing federal lands.

Federal, state, and local respondents also pointed to a number of federal laws as assisting adaptation efforts. For example, multiple officials cited the Global Change Research Act of 1990, which established a federal interagency research program to assist the United States and the world to understand, assess, predict, and respond to human-induced and natural processes of global change. Officials from the New York City Panel on Climate Change credited the 2001 Metro East Coast report issued for USGCRP with increasing awareness of regional climate change effects, which led to local government response.[72] Multiple officials also said that the National Environmental Policy Act could assist adaptation efforts by

---

[71]GAO, *Climate Change: Expert Opinion on the Economics of Policy Options to Address Climate Change*, GAO-08-605 (Washington, D.C.: May 9, 2008).

[72]Columbia Earth Institute, *Climate Change and a Global City: The Potential Consequences of Climate Variability and Change Metro East Coast*, a special report prepared at the request of the U.S. Global Change Research Program, July 2001.

incorporating climate change adaptation into the assessment process. According to CEQ officials, the federal government could provide adaptation information under the National Environmental Policy Act provision that directs all federal agencies to make available to states, counties, municipalities, and others advice and information useful in restoring, maintaining, and enhancing the quality of the environment. According to certain officials, the Coastal Zone Management Act, which is administered by NOAA, could encourage adaptation to climate change at the state and local levels by allowing states and territories to develop specific coastal climate change plans or strategies. The state of Maryland is already using Coastal Zone Management Act programs to assess and respond to the risk of sea level rise and coastal hazards.

Guidance on how to consider adaptation in existing processes: Nearly 66 percent (118 of 180) of respondents rated the "issuance of guidance, policies, or procedures on how to incorporate adaptation into existing policy and management processes" as very or extremely useful. A federal respondent added that adapting to climate change means integrating adaptation strategies into the programs that are already ongoing and will rely upon the networks and institutions that already exist. These sentiments were echoed in a recent report, which suggested that the experience of deliberately incorporating climate adaptation into projects can be very helpful in developing a more systematic approach to adaptation planning and can serve as a kind of project-based policy development.[73] Furthermore, this report notes that leading programs integrate climate change adaptation into overarching policy documents such as official plans or policies. In the same vein, King County officials told us they work to "routinize" climate change into planning decisions and have incorporated climate change into the county's comprehensive plan. This plan, among other things, states that "King County should consider projected impacts of climate change, including more severe winter flooding, when updating disaster preparedness, levee investment, and land use plans, as well as development regulations."[74] Several respondents cautioned that federal guidance related to adaptation should be flexible enough to allow state and local governments to adapt their own approaches.

---

[73]The Clean Air Partnership, *Cities Preparing for Climate Change: A Study of Six Urban Regions* (May 2007).

[74]King County, *King County Comprehensive Plan 2008.*

Governmentwide Planning and Collaboration Could Assist Adaptation Efforts

Climate change is a complex, interdisciplinary issue with the potential to affect every sector and level of government operations. Strategic planning is a way to respond to this governmentwide problem on a governmentwide scale. Our past work on crosscutting issues suggests that governmentwide strategic planning can integrate activities that span a wide array of federal, state, and local entities.[75] Strategic planning can also provide a comprehensive framework for considering organizational changes, making resource decisions, and holding officials accountable for achieving real and sustainable results.

As this report and others demonstrate, some communities and federal lands are already seeing the effects of climate change, and governments are beginning to respond.[76] However, as this report also illustrates, the federal government's emerging adaptation activities are carried out in an ad hoc manner and are not well coordinated across federal agencies, let alone state and local governments. Officials who responded to our questionnaire at all levels of government said that they face a range of challenges when considering adaptation efforts, including competing priorities, lack of site-specific data, and lack of clear roles and responsibilities. These officials also identified a number of potential federal actions that they thought could help address these challenges.

Multiple federal agencies, as well as state and local governments, will have to work together to address these challenges and implement new initiatives. Yet, our past work on collaboration among federal agencies suggests that they will face a range of barriers in doing so.[77] Agency missions may not be mutually reinforcing or may even conflict with each other, making consensus on strategies and priorities difficult. Incompatible procedures, processes, data, and computer systems also hinder collaboration. The resulting patchwork of programs and actions can waste scarce funds and limit the overall effectiveness of the federal

---

[75]GAO, *A Call For Stewardship: Enhancing the Federal Government's Ability to Address Key Fiscal and Other 21st Century Challenges*, GAO-08-93SP (Washington, D.C.: Dec. 17, 2007).

[76]GAO, *Alaska Native Villages: Limited Progress Has Been Made on Relocating Villages Threatened by Flooding and Erosion*, GAO-09-551 (Washington, D.C.: June 3, 2009), and GAO-07-863.

[77]GAO, *Results-Oriented Government: Practices That Can Help Enhance and Sustain Collaboration among Federal Agencies*, GAO-06-15 (Washington, D.C.: Oct. 21, 2005), and *Managing for Results: Barriers to Interagency Coordination*, GAO/GGD-00-106 (Washington, D.C.: Mar. 29, 2000).

effort. In addition, many federal programs were designed decades ago to address earlier challenges, informed by the conditions, technologies, management models, and organizational structures of past eras.[78] Based on our prior work, key practices that can help agencies enhance and sustain their collaborative efforts include[79]

- defining and articulating a common outcome;

- agreeing on roles and responsibilities;

- establishing compatible policies, procedures, and other means to operate across agency boundaries;

- identifying and addressing needs by leveraging resources; and

- developing mechanisms to monitor, evaluate, and report on results.

As we have previously reported, perhaps the single most important element of successful management improvement initiatives is the demonstrated commitment of top leaders to change.[80] Top leadership involvement and clear lines of accountability are critical to overcoming natural resistance to change, marshalling needed resources, and building and maintaining the commitment to new ways of doing business.

Conclusions

A key question for decision makers in both Congress and the administration is whether to start adapting now or to wait until the effects of climate change are more obvious and widespread. Given the complexity and potential magnitude of climate change and the lead time needed to adapt, preparing for these impacts now may reduce the need for far more costly steps in the decades to come.

Adaptation, however, will require making policy and management decisions that cut across traditional sectors, issues, and jurisdictional boundaries. It will mean developing new approaches to match new

---

[78]GAO, *21st Century Challenges: Reexamining the Base of the Federal Government*, GAO-05-325SP (Washington, D.C.: Feb. 1, 2005).

[79]GAO-06-15.

[80]GAO, *Management Reform: Elements of Successful Improvement Initiatives*, GAO/T-GGD-00-26 (Washington, D.C.: Oct. 15, 1999).

GAO-10-113 Climate Change Adaptation

realities. Old ways of doing business—such as making decisions based on the assumed continuation of past climate conditions—will not work in a world affected by climate change.

Certain state and local authorities on the "front lines" of early adaptation efforts understand this new reality and are beginning to take action. Our analysis of these efforts, responses to our questionnaire, and available studies revealed that federal, state, and local officials face numerous challenges when considering adaptation efforts. To be effective, federal efforts to address these challenges must be coordinated and directed toward a common goal.

Recommendations for Executive Action

We recommend that the appropriate entities within the Executive Office of the President, such as the Council on Environmental Quality and the Office of Science and Technology Policy, in consultation with relevant federal agencies, state and local governments, and key congressional committees of jurisdiction, develop a national strategic plan that will guide the nation's efforts to adapt to a changing climate. The plan should, among other things, (1) define federal priorities related to adaptation; (2) clarify roles, responsibilities, and working relationships among federal, state, and local governments; (3) identify mechanisms to increase the capacity of federal, state, and local agencies to incorporate information about current and potential climate change impacts into government decision making; (4) address how resources will be made available to implement the plan; and (5) build on and integrate ongoing federal planning efforts related to adaptation.

Agency Comments and Our Evaluation

We provided a draft of this report to the Council on Environmental Quality (CEQ), within the Executive Office of the President, for review and comment. CEQ circulated the report to the climate change adaptation interagency committee—including representatives from more than 12 agencies—for review and comment. In written comments, CEQ's Deputy Associate Director for Climate Change Adaptation generally agreed with the recommendations of the report, noting that leadership and coordination is necessary within the federal government to ensure an effective and appropriate adaptation response and that such coordination would help to catalyze regional, state, and local activities. These comments are reproduced in appendix IV. CEQ also provided technical comments, which we incorporated, as appropriate.

With regard to the report's findings, the Deputy Associate Director stated that CEQ had three main areas of concern. First, CEQ expressed concern that the relative inexperience of the federal government on adaptation combined with the methodology used in this report may produce misleading results. Specifically, the Deputy Associate Director stated that the report documents the relatively low level of activity within the federal government on adaptation, suggesting that most federal government respondents must be relatively inexperienced with adaptation issues. The Deputy Associate Director further stated that this relative federal inexperience may call some of our findings into question, citing as an example that the variability and local nature of adaptation makes a federally produced list of "no regrets" actions very difficult and possibly of limited utility. CEQ noted that, while the questionnaire results are an accurate reflection of the respondents' thinking, they do not necessarily paint the best roadmap for federal government action.

We do not agree with the characterization of federal officials as less experienced with adaptation issues than their state and local counterparts. As noted in the report scope and methodology (see app. I), we administered a Web-based questionnaire to a nonprobability sample of 274 federal, state, and local officials who were identified by their organizations to be knowledgeable about climate change adaptation. The officials who responded represent a diverse array of disciplines, including planners, scientists, and public health professionals. In general, the information we collected with the questionnaire suggests that the federal, state, and local officials who responded spend similar amounts of time on adaptation-related issues. We found that, in several instances, the state and local officials who were knowledgeable about adaptation worked very closely with their federal counterparts. Furthermore, regarding CEQ's specific example of federally produced "no regrets" lists, as we point out in this report, we agree that adaptation actions need to reflect local realities. However, questionnaire results were never intended to provide a roadmap specifically for federal activities but instead to describe the views of federal, state, and local officials on the potential federal actions (previously cited in available literature) that would be most useful to them. This information could be helpful when developing a strategy, but was not intended to be the strategy. We acknowledge that efforts to pursue these actions would often be collaborative, involving state and local entities.

Second, CEQ expressed concern that the report confuses the issue of cost-benefit analysis and scientific uncertainty, noting that the report identifies "justifying current costs with limited information about future benefits" as a challenge to adaptation policy, although the discussion of this challenge focuses on the scientific uncertainty inherent in climate projections as the main stumbling block for cost-benefit analysis. The Deputy Associate Director also noted that this section of the report did not include other challenges identified in the questionnaire, such as "understanding costs and benefits" of adaptive actions, or the challenge of prioritizing adaptation against other near-term actions and that cost-benefit analysis is a separate concern to scientific uncertainty.

Although we recognize CEQ's concern about this section of the report, we note that the report describes the link between scientific uncertainty and cost-benefit analysis and that the report describes many challenges other than scientific uncertainty. Uncertainty, scientific or otherwise, is generally incorporated into cost-benefit analysis as a best practice. We also note that the challenges and potential federal actions described in this report are closely related. As described in the subsequent section, for example, local impacts must be translated into costs and benefits, since this information is required for many decision-making processes. Almost 70 percent (126 of 180) of the respondents to our questionnaire rated "understanding the costs and benefits of adaptation efforts" as very or extremely challenging.

Finally, CEQ expressed concern that the report does not focus enough on implementation challenges, stating that the report does not analyze the primary barriers or challenges to implementation, or make any recommendations on implementing adaptation. The Deputy Associate Director acknowledged that planning is critical, but that it does not guarantee implementation and that implementation challenges are neither discussed nor developed in the report.

We agree that planning does not guarantee implementation and note that many of the challenges explored in this report relate to implementation. However, wide-scale implementation of adaptive actions before deriving a reasoned plan strikes us as "putting the cart before the horse." Without adequate planning at the federal level to chart a roadmap that, among other things, defines a common outcome and sets roles and responsibilities, it will be more difficult for multiple federal agencies, as well as state and local governments to work together to devise, much less execute, an implementation strategy.

As agreed with your office, unless you publicly announce the contents of this report earlier, we plan no further distribution until 30 days from the report date. At that time, we will send copies to the Chair of the Council on Environmental Quality and other interested parties. The report also will be available at no charge on the GAO Web site at http://www.gao.gov.

If you or your staff have any questions about this report, please contact me at (202) 512-3841 or stephensonj@gao.gov. Contact points for our Offices of Congressional Relations and Public Affairs may be found on the last page of this report. GAO staff who made major contributions to this report are listed in appendix V.

Sincerely yours,

John B. Stephenson
Director
Natural Resources and Environment

Appendix I: Scope and Methodology

Our review (1) determines what actions, if any, federal, state, local, and international authorities are taking to adapt to a changing climate; (2) identifies the challenges, if any, that federal, state, and local officials reported facing in their efforts to adapt; and (3) identifies actions that Congress and federal agencies could take to help address these challenges. We also provide information about our prior work on responding to similarly complex, interdisciplinary issues.

To determine the actions federal authorities are taking to adapt to climate change, we obtained summaries of current and planned adaptation-related efforts from a broad range of federal agencies. Full summaries from federal agencies are provided in a supplement to this report (see GAO-10-114SP). We obtained these summaries from the federal agencies with assistance from the U.S. Global Change Research Program (USGCRP), formerly the United States Climate Change Science Program. USGCRP coordinates and integrates federal research on changes in the global environment and their implications for society. USGCRP collected submissions from 12 of the 13 departments and agencies that participate in its program (see app. II for more details).[1]

We also obtained a summary of adaptation-related efforts from the Federal Emergency Management Agency, part of the U.S. Department of Homeland Security, as a follow up to prior GAO work on climate change and the Federal Emergency Management Agency's National Flood Insurance Program. Because the U.S. Department of Homeland Security is not part of USGCRP, we solicited its submission directly.

Because we wanted to include current federal activities that the agencies themselves consider to be related to adaptation, we did not modify the content of these summaries, except to remove references to specific individuals. We also did not independently confirm the information in the summaries. In addition, because the request for summaries was made to a select group of federal agencies, the activities compiled in this report should not be considered a comprehensive list of all recent and ongoing climate change adaptation efforts across the federal government.

In addition to gathering summaries, we also conducted an Internet search to identify other federal, state, or local organizations that are taking action to adapt to a changing climate. This search also helped to identify

---

[1]We did not receive a submission from the Smithsonian Institution.

challenges agencies face in their efforts to adapt, as well as actions the federal government could take, which are relevant to our second and third objectives. We searched the Web sites of relevant organizations and agencies, such as the Intergovernmental Panel on Climate Change, the Pew Center on Global Climate Change, the Coastal States Organization, and federal agencies such as the Environmental Protection Agency and the National Oceanic and Atmospheric Administration. We also conducted Internet searches using relevant key words, such as "climate change" and "climate change adaptation." We reviewed publicly available English-language documents related to adaptation efforts in the United States and other countries that we identified through our search.

To address our three objectives, we also conducted 13 open-ended interviews with a select group of organizations and agencies that are engaged in climate change adaptation activities. We selected them based on their level of involvement in the issue of climate change adaptation, as determined by (1) previous GAO work; (2) scoping interviews (a "snowball" technique); and (3) our search of the background literature. We attempted to speak with organizations that are working on climate change adaptation, as well as those that represent sectors affected by it. We generally focused on organizations and sectors that are working on this issue on a national level (rather than just in one city or region) and that have also worked closely with state and local officials. The organizations included the National Association of Clean Water Agencies, the H. John Heinz III Center for Science, Economics, and the Environment, ICLEI—Local Governments for Sustainability, and the Nature Conservancy, among others. In addition, we spoke with two academics who had a long-standing involvement with climate change issues at the national and international levels to gather additional background information on the issue. Because we spoke with a select group of organizations and individuals, we cannot generalize our results to those we did not interview.

In addition to asking our interviewees about the actions they are taking to address adaptation, we also asked them to identify other relevant reports or studies we should include in our work and other agencies or organizations that are engaged in adaptation activities (part of our "snowball" technique). We also asked what actions they thought the federal government and Congress could take to help in their efforts.

To determine the actions federal, state, local, and international authorities are taking to adapt to a changing climate, we also visited four sites where government officials are taking actions to adapt. We chose these sites because they were frequently mentioned in the background literature and scoping interviews as examples of locations that are implementing climate change adaptation and which may offer particularly useful insights into the types of actions governments can take to plan for climate change impacts. These sites are neither comprehensive nor representative of all state and local climate change adaptation efforts. They include New York City; King County, Washington; the state of Maryland; and the United Kingdom, focusing on the London region. We included an international site visit to examine how other countries are starting to adapt, and we specifically selected the United Kingdom because its climate change adaptation efforts were mentioned frequently in the background literature and scoping interviews and because it had already begun to implement these efforts at the national, regional, and local levels. During our site visits, we gathered information through interviews with officials and stakeholders, observation of adaptation efforts, and reviewed related documents. We also followed up with officials after our visits to gather additional information.

To describe the challenges that federal, state, and local officials face in their efforts to adapt and the potential actions that Congress and federal agencies could take to help address these challenges, we administered a Web-based questionnaire to a nonprobability sample of 274 federal, state, and local officials who were identified by their organizations to be knowledgeable about adaptation. To identify relevant potential respondents, we worked with organizations that represent federal, state, and local officials. Specifically, we worked with organizations such as USGCRP (federal), National Association of Clean Air Agencies (state), and Conference of Mayors (local), among others, and asked them to identify officials who are knowledgeable about climate change adaptation. These officials were generally identified through their involvement in climate change working groups within these organizations, which indicated a level of interest and knowledge of the issue. The officials were then contacted by their organization to describe the purpose of our questionnaire and to ask if they would participate. The names and e-mail addresses of those who agreed were then provided to GAO. The federal, state, and local officials who responded represent a diverse array of disciplines, including planners, scientists, and public health professionals; however, their responses cannot be generalized to officials who did not complete our questionnaire.

To develop the questionnaire, information was compiled from background literature and interviews we conducted with relevant organizations and officials. Using this information, we developed lists of challenges and potential actions the federal government could take to address them.

Using closed-ended questions, respondents were asked to rate several challenges and actions on 5 point Likert scales (the closed-ended questions are reproduced in app. III). We also included open-ended questions to give respondents an opportunity to tell us about challenges and potential federal actions that we did not ask about. Lastly, we included additional open-ended questions to gather opinions on a small number of related topics.

Because this was not a sample survey, it has no sampling errors. However, the practical difficulties of conducting any questionnaire may introduce errors, commonly known as nonsampling errors. For example, difficulties in interpreting a particular question, sources of information available to respondents, or analyzing data can introduce unwanted variability in the results. We took steps to minimize such nonsampling errors.

For example, social science survey specialists designed the questionnaire in collaboration with GAO staff who had subject matter expertise. Then, we sent a draft of the questionnaire to several federal, state, and local organizations for comment. In addition, we pretested it with local, state, and federal officials to check that (1) the questions were clear and unambiguous, (2) terminology was used correctly, (3) the questionnaire did not place an undue burden on agency officials, and (4) the questionnaire was comprehensive and unbiased. Based on these steps, we made necessary corrections and edits before it was administered. When we analyzed the data, an independent analyst checked all computer programs. Since this was a Web-based instrument, respondents entered their answers directly into the electronic questionnaire, eliminating the need to key data into a database, minimizing error.

We developed and administered a Web-based questionnaire accessible through a secure server. When we completed the final questionnaire, including content and form, we sent an e-mail announcement of the questionnaire to our nonprobability sample of 274 federal, state, and local officials on May 13, 2009. They were notified that the questionnaire was available online and were given unique passwords and usernames on May 28, 2009. We sent follow-up e-mail messages on June 4, June 8, and June 12, 2009, to those who had not yet responded. Then we contacted the remaining nonrespondents by telephone to encourage them to complete the questionnaire online, starting on June 24, 2009. The questionnaire was available online until July 10, 2009. Questionnaires were completed by 187 officials, for a response rate of about 68 percent.[2] The response rate by level of government is about 82 percent for federal officials (72 out of 88), about 90 percent for state officials (47 out of 52), and about 50 percent (65 out of 131) for local officials.[3]

We presented our questionnaire results in six tables in our report, which show the relative rankings of the challenges and potential actions listed in our questionnaire based on the percentage of respondents that rated them very or extremely challenging (for challenges) or very or extremely useful (for potential actions). Both the challenges and potential actions are organized into groups related to the following: (1) awareness and priorities, (2) information, and (3) the structure and operation of the federal government. Tables showing more detailed summaries of federal, state, and local officials' responses to the questionnaire are included in appendix III.

We conducted this performance audit from September 2008 to October 2009 in accordance with generally accepted government auditing standards. Those standards require that we plan and perform the audit to obtain sufficient, appropriate evidence to provide a reasonable basis for our findings and conclusions based on our audit objectives. We believe that the evidence obtained provides a reasonable basis for our findings and conclusions based on our audit objectives.

---

[2] Not all officials responded to every question.

[3] Three officials from levels of government other than federal, state, or local—such as a regional level—also responded to the questionnaire.

Appendix II: Information on Selected Federal Efforts to Adapt to a Changing Climate

We obtained information from 13 selected federal departments and agencies on their current and planned climate change adaptation efforts. We present this information in a supplement to this report to provide a more complete picture of the activities that federal agencies consider to be related to climate change adaptation than has been available publicly (see GAO-10-114SP). We obtained this information directly from the agencies participating in the U.S. Global Change Research Program.[1]

Importantly, we did not modify the content of the agency submissions (except to remove references to named individuals) or assess its validity. In addition, because this information represents the efforts of a selected group of federal agencies, the agency activities compiled in the supplement should not be considered a comprehensive list of all recent and ongoing climate change adaptation efforts across the federal government. Any questions about the information presented in the supplement should be directed to the agencies themselves.

See the following list for the departments and agencies included in the supplement to this report:

U.S. Department of Agriculture

- Agricultural Marketing Service
- Agricultural Research Service
- Cooperative State Research, Education, and Extension Service
- Economic Research Service
- Farm Service Agency
- Forest Service
- Natural Resources Conservation Service

U.S. Department of Commerce

- National Oceanic and Atmospheric Administration

---

[1]The U.S. Global Change Research Program (USGCRP) coordinates and integrates federal research on changes in the global environment and their implications for society. We did not receive a submission from the Smithsonian Institution. In addition to the agencies that participate in USGCRP, we also obtained a summary of current and planned adaptation-related efforts from the Federal Emergency Management Agency, part of the U.S. Department of Homeland Security, because of prior GAO adaptation-related work on its National Flood Insurance Program.

U.S. Department of Defense

- Office of the Secretary of Defense
- Army
- Navy
- Air Force
- Marine Corps
- U.S. Army Corps of Engineers

U.S. Department of Energy

U.S. Department of Health and Human Services

- Centers for Disease Control and Prevention
- National Institutes of Health

U.S. Department of Homeland Security

- Federal Emergency Management Agency

U.S. Department of the Interior

U.S. Department of State and U.S. Agency for International Development

U.S. Department of Transportation

- Office of Transportation Policy

U.S. Environmental Protection Agency

National Aeronautics and Space Administration

National Science Foundation

Table 8: All Officials' Rating of Challenges Related to Awareness and Priorities

How challenging are each of the following for officials when considering climate change adaptation efforts?

	(1) Not at all	(2) Slightly	(3) Moderately	(4) Very	(5) Extremely	Not applicable	Don't know/no response	Total responses[a]	Average[b]
Lack of funding for adaptation efforts	0	4	25	43	107	1	3	183	4.41
Non-adaptation activities are higher priorities	4	15	33	62	66	5	1	186	3.95
Lack of clear priorities for allocating resources for adaptation activities	3	12	39	71	56	2	3	186	3.91
Lack of public awareness or knowledge of adaptation	0	20	51	83	30	0	2	186	3.67
Lack of awareness or knowledge of adaptation among government officials	2	17	58	74	31	0	2	184	3.63
Difficult to define adaptation goals and performance metrics	1	21	58	66	35	0	5	186	3.62
Lack of qualified staff to work on adaptation efforts	5	25	60	44	47	0	5	186	3.57
Lack of a specific mandate to address climate change adaptation	18	24	35	50	55	2	2	186	3.55
Lack of clarity about what activities are considered adaptation	3	19	59	79	21	2	2	185	3.53

Source: GAO.

[a]The total column represents the number of officials who answered each question out of the 187 respondents that completed the questionnaire.

[b]The average column represents the average of the numerical ratings submitted by officials for (1) not at all challenging through (5) extremely challenging.

Table 9: All Officials' Rating of Challenges Related to Information

How challenging are each of the following for officials when considering climate change adaptation efforts?

	(1) Not at all	(2) Slightly	(3) Moderately	(4) Very	(5) Extremely	Not applicable	Don't know/no response	Total responses[a]	Average[b]
Size and complexity of *future* climate change impacts	1	8	33	65	73	1	4	185	4.12
Justifying the current costs of adaptation efforts for potentially less certain future benefits	1	7	29	76	66	2	4	185	4.11
Translating available climate information (e.g., projected temperature, precipitation) into impacts at the local level (e.g., increased stream flow)	3	13	30	62	74	1	2	185	4.05
Availability of climate information at relevant scale (i.e., downscaled regional and local information)	4	15	27	66	67	0	4	183	3.99
Understanding the costs and benefits of adaptation efforts	0	5	49	78	48	2	3	185	3.94
Making management and policy decisions with uncertainty about future effects of climate change	2	14	50	68	50	0	1	185	3.82
Lack of information about thresholds (i.e., limits beyond which recovery is impossible or difficult)	7	17	38	66	47	3	7	185	3.74
Lack of baseline monitoring data to enable evaluation of adaptation actions (i.e., inability to detect change)	7	17	44	78	35	1	2	184	3.65
Lack of certainty about the timing of climate change impacts	3	16	58	68	35	0	3	183	3.64

How challenging are each of the following for officials when considering climate change adaptation efforts?

	(1) Not at all	(2) Slightly	(3) Moderately	(4) Very	(5) Extremely	Not applicable	Don't know/no response	Total responses[a]	Average[b]
Accessibility and usability of available information on climate impacts and adaptation	6	25	54	64	33	0	2	184	3.51
Size and complexity of *current* climate change impacts	6	22	64	56	31	1	4	184	3.47

Source: GAO.

[a]The total column represents the number of officials who answered each question out of the 187 respondents that completed the questionnaire.

[b]The average column represents the average of the numerical ratings submitted by officials for (1) not at all challenging through (5) extremely challenging.

Table 10: All Officials' Rating of Challenges Related to the Structure and Operation of the Federal Government

How challenging are each of the following for officials when considering climate change adaptation efforts?

	(1) Not at all	(2) Slightly	(3) Moderately	(4) Very	(5) Extremely	Not applicable	Don't know/no response	Total responses[a]	Average[b]
Lack of clear roles and responsibilities for addressing adaptation across all levels of government (i.e., adaptation is everyone's problem but nobody's direct responsibility)	4	16	34	54	70	2	5	185	3.96
The authority and capability to adapt is spread among many federal agencies (i.e., institutional fragmentation)	4	23	47	66	36	2	7	185	3.61
Lack of federal guidance or policies on how to make decisions related to adaptation	11	22	51	53	39	3	6	185	3.49
Existing federal policies, programs, or practices that hinder adaptation efforts	8	31	47	30	34	3	31	184	3.34
Federal statutory, regulatory, or other legal constraints on adaptation efforts	14	33	50	29	26	4	29	185	3.13

Source: GAO.

[a]The total column represents the number of officials who answered each question out of the 187 respondents that completed the questionnaire.

[b]The average column represents the average of the numerical ratings submitted by officials for (1) not at all challenging through (5) extremely challenging.

Table 11: All Officials' Rating of Potential Federal Government Actions Related to Awareness and Priorities

How useful, if at all, would each of the following federal government actions be for officials in efforts to adapt to a changing climate?

	(1) Not at all	(2) Slightly	(3) Moderately	(4) Very	(5) Extremely	Don't know/no response	Total responses[a]	Average[b]
Development of regional or local educational workshops for relevant officials that are tailored to their responsibilities	3	7	36	64	72	2	184	4.07
Development of lists of "no regrets" actions (i.e., actions in which the benefits exceed the costs under all future climate scenarios)	4	13	31	60	73	5	186	4.02
Creation of a campaign to educate the public about climate change adaptation	1	19	35	60	69	0	184	3.96
Development of a list of potential climate change adaptation policy options	2	12	38	73	56	4	185	3.93
Training of relevant officials on adaptation issues	3	14	38	69	58	2	184	3.91
Creation of a recurring stakeholder forum to explore the interaction of climate science and adaptation practice	3	21	41	70	49	2	186	3.77
Prioritization of potential climate change adaptation options	9	19	42	70	43	3	186	3.65

Source: GAO.

[a]The total column represents the number of officials who answered each question out of the 187 respondents that completed the questionnaire.

[b]The average column represents the average of the numerical ratings submitted by officials for (1) not at all useful through (5) extremely useful.

Table 12: All Officials' Rating of Potential Federal Government Actions Related to Information

How useful, if at all, would each of the following federal government actions be for officials in efforts to adapt to a changing climate?

	(1) Not at all	(2) Slightly	(3) Moderately	(4) Very	(5) Extremely	Don't know/no response	Total responses[a]	Average[b]
Development of *state and local* climate change impact and vulnerability assessments	2	9	25	56	91	1	184	4.23
Development of *regional* climate change impact and vulnerability assessments	0	5	36	60	81	3	185	4.19
Development of processes and tools to help officials access, interpret, and apply available climate information	0	7	30	72	76	0	185	4.17
Identification and sharing of best practices	0	7	24	65	61	2	159[c]	4.15
Creation of a federal service to consolidate and deliver climate information to decision makers to inform adaptation efforts	11	20	38	41	66	9	185	3.74
Development of an interactive stakeholder forum for information sharing	1	23	56	58	46	1	185	3.68

Source: GAO.

[a]The total column represents the number of officials who answered each question out of the 187 respondents that completed the questionnaire.

[b]The average column represents the average of the numerical ratings submitted by officials for (1) not at all useful through (5) extremely useful.

[c]As previously noted, 187 respondents completed our questionnaire overall. While the number of responses for each individual question generally ranged from 183 to 186, only 159 respondents answered this question.

Table 13: All Officials' Rating of Potential Federal Government Actions Related to the Structure and Operation of the Federal Government

How useful, if at all, would each of the following federal government actions be for officials in efforts to adapt to a changing climate?

	(1) Not at all	(2) Slightly	(3) Moderately	(4) Very	(5) Extremely	Don't know/no response	Total responses[a]	Average[b]
Development of a national adaptation fund to provide a consistent funding stream for adaptation activities	7	8	13	38	113	5	184	4.35
Development of a national adaptation strategy that defines federal government priorities and respons bilities	4	12	36	65	64	4	185	3.96
Review of existing programs to identify and modify policies and practices that hinder adaptation efforts	1	19	38	65	57	5	185	3.88
Issuance of guidance, policies, or procedures on how to incorporate adaptation into existing policy and management processes	2	15	45	78	40	4	184	3.77
Development of a climate change extension service to help share and explain available information	8	20	46	54	53	3	184	3.69
Creation of a centralized government structure to coordinate adaptation funding	24	20	33	44	45	19	185	3.40

Source: GAO.

[a]The total column represents the number of officials who answered each question out of the 187 respondents that completed the questionnaire.

[b]The average column represents the average of the numerical ratings submitted by officials for (1) not at all useful through (5) extremely useful.

Appendix IV: Comments from the Council on Environmental Quality

EXECUTIVE OFFICE OF THE PRESIDENT
COUNCIL ON ENVIRONMENTAL QUALITY
WASHINGTON, D.C. 20503

John B. Stephenson
Director
Natural Resources and Environment
U.S. Government Accountability Office
441 G Street N.W.
Washington, DC 20548

Dear Mr. Stephenson,

Thank you for the opportunity to review and comment on Government Accountability Office's report, "Climate Change Adaptation: Strategic Federal Planning Could Help Government Officials Make More Informed Decisions." We circulated the report to the Climate Change Adaptation inter-agency committee for review and comment. The committee includes representatives from more than twelve agencies. We have also provided technical comments under separate cover.

We agree that adaptation is a critical area for federal government activity and think this report is a timely review of the subject. Overall, we agree with the main recommendation, that leadership and coordination is necessary within the federal government to ensure an effective and appropriate adaptation response. Further, we agree that this will help to catalyze the local, state and regional activities that are so critical to adaptation.

We have three main areas of concern with the report. First, we believe that the relative inexperience of the federal government on adaptation combined with the survey methodology used in this report may produce misleading results. Second, we believe that the report confuses the issue of cost/benefit analysis and scientific uncertainty. Third, we think the overall report does not focus enough on implementation challenges and recommendations.

Methodology
The report uses a survey methodology to assess relative roles and tasks for the federal government on adaptation. Survey respondents were selected from both within and outside the federal government, and all had experience with adaptation. However, the report also documents the relatively low level of activity within the federal government on adaptation, suggesting that most federal government respondents must be relatively inexperienced with adaptation issues. This is reinforced by the significant differences in some survey responses between respondents within the federal government, and those with presumably greater adaptation experience, outside of the federal government.

As a result, some of the survey findings appear to be questionable. For example, the survey found that developing a list of no-regrets actions would be a valuable product for the federal government to produce. While no-regrets actions are a critical part of adaptation, the variability and local nature of adaptation makes a federally produced list of no-regrets actions very difficult and possibly of limited utility. Therefore, while the

EXECUTIVE OFFICE OF THE PRESIDENT
COUNCIL ON ENVIRONMENTAL QUALITY
WASHINGTON, D.C. 20503

survey results are an accurate reflection of respondents thinking, they do not necessarily paint the best roadmap for federal government action.

Cost/Benefit and Uncertainty

The report identifies "justifying current costs with limited information about future benefits" as a challenge to adaptation policy. The discussion of this challenge focuses on the scientific uncertainty inherent in climate projections as the main stumbling block for cost/benefit analysis. The section does not include other challenges identified in the survey, such as "understanding costs and benefits" of adaptive actions, or the challenge of prioritizing adaptation against other near-term actions. The survey written comments point out that given the scientific uncertainty on impacts, cost/benefit analysis is particularly important. In these cases, cost/benefit analysis is a separate concern to scientific uncertainty.

Our interpretation of these survey responses is that while scientific uncertainty is a concern and challenge for adaptation planning and implementation, there is also difficulty doing cost/benefit analysis. This difficulty could be addressed through providing decision-maker tools, like scenario analyses, and tools that help to quantify the cost and benefits of inaction and action.

Planning vs. Implementation

The recommendation focuses on 4 components of a national strategic adaptation plan: priorities, roles and responsibilities, information and planning. These are critical elements of a national strategy on adaptation, and respond to the main challenges identified in the report.

However, the report does not analyze the primary barriers or challenges to implementation, nor does make any recommendations on implementing adaptation. Experience to date on adaptation suggests that planning is critical, but that it does not guarantee implementation. Many of the challenges described in the survey could apply equally to implementation (e.g., public awareness) and some were specifically focused on implementation (e.g., funding). But implementation challenges are neither discussed nor developed in the report. Simply fulfilling the recommendations on planning will not be sufficient to help the US adapt to climate change.

Thank you for the opportunity to review this report prior to its publication.

Sincerely,

Maria Blair
Deputy Associate Director for Climate Change Adaptation

Appendix V: GAO Contact and Staff Acknowledgments

GAO Contact	John B. Stephenson, (202) 512-3841 or stephensonj@gao.gov
Staff Acknowledgments	In addition to the contact named above, Steve Elstein (Assistant Director), Charles Bausell, Keya Chateauneuf, Cindy Gilbert, William Jenkins, Richard Johnson, Kirsten Lauber, Ty Mitchell, Benjamin Shouse, Jeanette Soares, Ruth Solomon, Kiki Theodoropoulos, and Joseph Thompson made key contributions to this report. Camille Adebayo, Holly Dye, Anne Johnson, Carol Kolarik, Jessica Lemke, Micah McMillan, Leah Probst, Jena Sinkfield, and Cynthia Taylor also made important contributions.